BREAKING BAD NEWS

SECOND EDITION

BREAKING BAD NEWS

ESSENTIAL TOOLS FOR CRISIS COMMUNICATION

JEFF HAHN

BREAKING BAD NEWS
Essential Tools for Crisis Communication

SECOND EDITION

ISBN   978-1-5445-5029-9   *Hardcover*
        978-1-5445-5028-2   *Paperback*
        978-1-5445-5030-5   *Ebook*

Library of Congress Cataloging-in-Publication Data Hahn, Jeffery L., author
Library of Congress Control Number: 2020902523 ISBN: 978-1-7345700-9-0
Book cover design by Butler

CONTENTS

INTRODUCTION

In the spring of 1992, I attended a two-day crisis management conference at the University of Nevada, Las Vegas as a member of the Motorola Semiconductor crisis management team. The room was filled with executives engaged in crisis management activities in major corporations and security firms and the agenda—ranging from personal security to the long-term effects of cell phone electromagnetic fields, to the strategies of anti-Silicon Valley activist groups—was of significant interest. On the second day of the conference, we were listening to a speaker talk in an animated fashion about the wisdom of the Chinese logogram pictured below.

The brush strokes on the top, he explained, symbolized the idea of crisis. Fluent Chinese speakers I have spoken with since then have, indeed, verified this conclusion. The symbol at the bottom, the speaker explained, implies opportunity. His point was that every crisis brings opportunity if we're willing to see it.

The general idea isn't new. When he was mayor of Chicago, Rahm Emanuel said, "You never let a serious crisis go to waste. And what I mean by that [is] it's an opportunity to do things you think you could not do before."[1] Saul Alinsky, the 1960s activist, talked about the same idea in his book, *Rules for Radicals*. Alinksy said, "In the arena of action, a threat or a crisis becomes almost a precondition to communication. Taking advantage of any crisis whether real or manufactured is a common tool used by those waging war in antithesis."[2]

The most likely origin for the notion is a 1959 speech President Kennedy gave in Indianapolis. A number of sources quote Kennedy as saying, "The Chinese use two brush strokes to write the word 'crisis.' One brush stroke stands for danger, the other for opportunity. In a crisis, be aware of the danger, but recognize the opportunity."[3]

Ted Sorensen was President Kennedy's speechwriter. For my money, he—along with William Safire (for Richard Nixon), Peggy Noonan (for Ronald Reagan), and Abraham Lincoln, himself—rank as the best speechwriters in our nation's history. Sorensen exercised some artistic latitude when he wrote the lines for Kennedy, and after digging into it, I discovered that more than a few scholars found Sorensen's interpretation wasn't exactly precise. Here's what Victor Mair, a professor of Chinese language and literature at the University of Pennsylvania, said about the interpretation:

[The symbol] wēijī indicates a perilous situation when one should be especially wary. It is not a juncture when one goes looking for advantages and benefits. In a crisis, one wants above all to save one's skin and neck! Any would-be guru who advocates opportunism in the face of crisis should be run out of town on a rail.[4]

I have always felt it was my obligation to guide my clients through a challenging moment with their reputation intact enough for opportunity to present itself, but only well after a crisis has passed. In thirty-plus years inside the war rooms of dozens of clients facing crises, not once have I emerged high-fiving my counterparts to celebrate the wonderful opportunity we had just been presented. Just the opposite, in fact. I'm usually emotionally wrung out.

When you see, as I did in 2002, a corpse—frozen in a crouched position behind a hazardous chemical truck, his hands gripping a valve wheel as if he was struck by a lightning bolt of ice—the word "opportunity" just doesn't spring to mind. Instead, you wonder what to communicate to the family of the deceased and then to the homeowners living in a subdivision just across the fence line from toxic agents that may have been released into the air near their children's bedrooms.

Crises suck. They're nerve-racking. They're high-stakes gut pretzels that have had me walking the floors at night on behalf of clients for decades. To anyone who tries to tell you a brand has emerged from a crisis better for the experience, you might want to remind them of the quote from Malcolm Forbes: "The dumbest people I know are those who know it all."

Crisis events are haunting. In my early career, I had the great privilege of working for Lockheed Space Operations. By the time I started my job at the Kennedy Space Center (KSC) in Florida, the Challenger accident was four years in the past. Still, for as long as I was there, the ghosts of that tragedy floated through the culture.

People spoke of Challenger in hushed tones about what had occurred, emotionally scarred by the lives lost and the political scorn heaped onto the space program in the hearings that followed. It's true that lessons were learned in the aftermath of Challenger. If you're a student of crisis management, a relentlessly thorough examination of the Challenger accident can be found in the book *No Downlink* by Claus Jensen. Jensen's analysis aside, my firsthand, after-the-fact observation of the dedicated team at KSC convinced me that crises create more scar tissue than blue sky.

The feeling and my resulting aversion to deep scars have motivated me to search for a way to help clients more successfully navigate crises. In the chapters that follow, I present a step-by-step method for doing just that within a constrained timeframe following a bad news break. The major components are these:

1. Activating your Rapid Response Team
2. Issuing holding statements
3. Developing crisis messaging
4. Selecting and preparing a messenger
5. Employing the best methods for message delivery

Along the way, I have done my best to attack complexity through a set of quick-to-understand tools that, with some practice, can be learned by anyone courageous enough to step into the ring of crisis communications.

The steps, and the tools accompanying each, make it fair to characterize this book as a study in rapid response tactics. Crisis strategists who prefer a shoot-from-the-hip approach might certainly agree. Dismissing tactics as trivial, however, is a mistake born from arrogance. Eric Rosenbach, former United States Pentagon Chief of Staff and Assistant Secretary of Defense for Homeland Defense and Global Security, put it this way: "Strategy without execution is hallucination."[5] Likewise, British Major General J.F.C. Fuller, a prolific strategist said this about tactics: "Tactics are the cutting edge of strategy, the edge which chisels out the plan in the action; consequently, the sharper this edge, the clearer cut will be the result."[6]

Breaking Bad News flows from these points-of-view. Its aim is to provide the reader a toolbox capable of illuminating how options are better than answers, and to pull away any assumptions or stereotypes about crisis communication being a dark-art.

CHAPTER 1

A TOOL COLLECTION JOURNEY

"The future's uncertain but the end is always near."

—JIM MORRISON

Seasoned reputation managers know it's not whether a crisis will occur for a brand, but when. In today's 24/7 news cycle world and troll-infested universe of social media instant outrage, it's virtually impossible to contain bad news. You're going to have to deal with it, so you had better be prepared to execute a strategy proportional to the speed and magnitude of unfolding events. This is especially true in complex industries where many opportunities exist for things to go wrong.

Throughout this book, I use many examples from a variety of business sectors because complexity is a constant companion for brands in every space, and bad news happens on a regular basis.

Start with the food and beverage sector as an example. In 1992 Perrier's benzene contamination incident was certainly bad news. The worldwide recall cost $250 million, and 750 people lost their jobs.[7] Likewise, when Cadbury-Schweppes recalled more than a million chocolate bars in 2006 due to salmonella poisoning in the

UK and Ireland, the company estimated the recall would cost more than $20 million.[8] Alcohol isn't immune to bad news either. In 2014, Fireball Cinnamon Whisky was recalled in Finland, Sweden, and Norway for containing antifreeze.[9]

These examples create a question with which any brand who values its reputation has to grapple: Can you shape the trajectory of bad news well enough to minimize reputational damage? I believe the answer is definitively yes, and that confidence forms the essence of this book.

The pages that follow focus on many types of bad news a brand can experience. We'll look at how one brand, caught up in a tsunami of negative publicity, took a devastating hit to its reputation by communicating poorly to its stakeholders...and the financial costs of that poor communication. Likewise, we'll give brands that have performed admirably in navigating crises the credit they deserve for reminding us how to muster clarity in foggy situations.

We begin our tool collection journey with a few baseline definitions. First, in reference to the title of this book, what is "bad news"? It is any news that is unexpected, unwelcome, disruptive, financially costly, and harmful to a brand's reputation. It is the news that knocks a company off strategy by requiring a dramatic response. How dramatic? Scott Galloway, a professor at New York University's Stern School of Business who is also a popular public speaker, author, podcast host, and entrepreneur, has a three-part recipe for responding to crises, which includes "overcorrecting." About this, he explains, "What's difficult about overreacting is it's disproportionate to the problem at present. It's deeply uncomfortable because you are devising a solution to a problem that doesn't yet exist and whose future scale you are guessing. Throwing vast resources at a guess is risky and hard to justify, yet if you wait long enough for the scale to unfold, it will be too late."[10]

The bad news talked about in this book also has one other characteristic: It leaves scars in the minds of the people—consumers and brand professionals—affected. Why? Because when an incident makes news, when it's public, it becomes a permanent, embarrassing, internet-searchable, monument to a brand's failure to anticipate, plan, or respond.

Brands experience challenging news on a regular basis. A change in leadership, a crummy review by an analyst, or even a poor earnings report might be viewed as bad news, but they don't typically cause emotional trauma. Real bad news is an event that leaves a lasting impression, creates negative memory, and alters the trajectory of a reputation.

Next, why does news break? Why do we call it "breaking news"? An etymologist named John Kelly, who occasionally writes for MashedRadish.com, researched the evolution of the term "breaking news." He found that the term *breaking*, as it relates to a news story becoming available to the public, emerged in the 1930s, and "fast-breaking news" by the 1940s. These uses of *break* convey "suddenly or surprisingly issuing or coming into notice or breaking forth. This 'bursting' sense of the verb break, invented in the early 1700s, ultimately suggests a literal rupture, i.e., breaking, of a metaphorical barrier, of knowledge, attention, or the like." Kelly's characterization of a piece of information becoming public is especially important. Without that one element, bad news hasn't broken, and a reputation isn't in peril.[11]

Finally, what do we mean when we say "reputation"? Warren Buffett talked about it when he said, "It takes twenty years to build a reputation and five minutes to ruin it."[12] Abraham Lincoln said, "Character is like a tree and reputation like its shadow. The shadow is what we think of it; the tree is the real thing."[13] These are memorable quotes, but they don't exactly give us an operating definition. I like what my friend Bill Coletti—a terrific reputation consultant— says about the question in his book, *Critical Moments*:

A reputation is made up of a series of critical moments that shape and mold it over an extended period. Reputation is ultimately based on the *expectation* of what a [brand] will do next, which is based on the public's perception of what the [brand] has done repeatedly over time. Past actions create an impression and set the stage for what people *expect* (emphasis mine) it to do next.[14]

The key word in Coletti's definition is "expectation." It is the foundation of the model presented later in the book, so it's worth emphasizing here. Your reputation is how your brand is seen by its stakeholders based on what they expect from you.

This thought has, in past conversations, created some controversy, but I believe it to be true: While you have complete agency to control your reputation, it is owned by the minds of people who have interacted with it in some way. They are the keepers of your reputation and the ones whose expectations create the perceptions that form your reputation.

I briefly touched on the link between reputation and financial cost. This deserves more attention as profits and reputation—one tangible, the other not—are linked. For some, this entanglement feels like bad news in and of itself, but a good reputation is often the deciding factor when a customer chooses one brand over another.[15]

With a good reputation, a company can elevate its product in a competitive marketplace and dominate with premium pricing. This is important, especially among belief-driven buyers, who see buying certain brands as a significant way to express themselves and tend to buy from companies aligned with their core beliefs. Uncertainty about the state of the world and distrust of traditional institutions like government fuel this phenomenon. Buying on belief is a fast track to a stronger consumer relationship. If a brand manages its reputation well and keeps it aligned with stakeholder expectations, its customers will be more loyal, more willing to pay a premium, and more willing to advocate for the brand. Two out of three global consumers today see themselves as belief-driven buyers.[16]

Crises of all types have similar characteristics—they are

sudden, they are public, and when they occur, they break with stakeholder expectations. They also follow a similar life cycle—a recognizable arc through which smart choices can be made and successful navigation achieved. The trouble is that the lifecycle descriptions are many and varied.

Author Steven Fink, for example, described crises as having four stages: prodromal, acute, chronic, and resolution.[17] Ian Mitroff divides crisis management into five stages: signal detection, probing and prevention, damage containment, recovery, and learning.[18] These make sense, but I like the quick clarity Chandler's Classic Crisis Stages Map provides. Robert C. Chandler is a retired university professor and crisis consultant. His model, the first tool for your toolbox, depicts the life cycle of a crisis as a series of overlapping stages, which is handy because it provides a "You Are Here" illustration.[19]

CHANDLER'S CLASSIC CRISIS STAGES MAP

Chandler's model enables us to see where we are in what is very likely a foggy situation making each stage worthy of a short explanation.

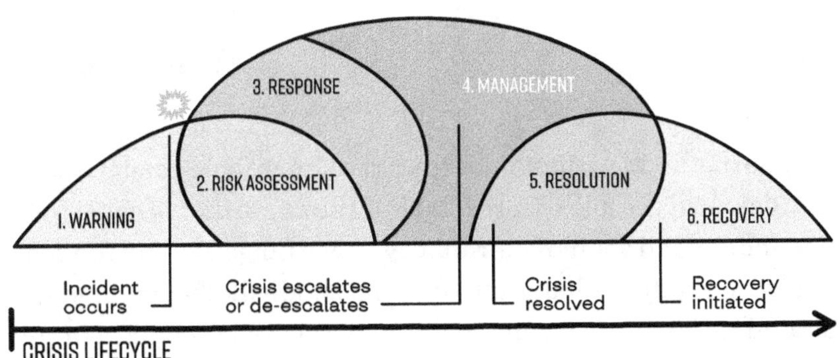

In the Warning stage, potential issues slope up from left to right. Crises can occur under conditions when there is a very distinct warning or none at all.

During the Risk Assessment phase, people weigh the potential consequences and damages of a crisis. I devised a tool you are welcome to put in your toolbox called the Cassandra Calculator™, shown below.

GOODWILL & ENGAGEMENT

The sentiment associated with a brand by external stakeholders and employees establishing "expected" and "normal" standards.

1	Very Positive/ High Expectations
2	Somewhat Positive
3	Neutral
4	Somewhat Negative
5	Negative/Low Expectations

TEAM READINESS

Established via the Readiness Diagnostic

1	Level 5	110+
2	Level 4	89–109
3	Level 3	68–88
4	Level 2	47–67
5	Level 1	26.5–46

SEVERITY

An event's potential consequences measured in terms of degree of damage, known insured losses, injury, or impact on mission. Should something go wrong, the results are likely to occur in:
• Death or injury
• Equipment damage
• Mission degradation
• Reduced morale
• Adverse publicity
• Administrative/ regulatory disciplinary action

1	None or slight
2	Minimal
3	Significant
4	Major
5	Catastrophic

EXPOSURE

The amount of time, # of occurrences, # of people and/or amount of equipment that would be involved in responding to an event, expressed in time, proximity, volume, or repetition.

1	Slight
2	Below average
3	Average
4	Above average
5	Significant

PROBABILITY

The likelihood that the potential consequences will occur.

1	Impossible/remote at any time
2	Unlikely in normal conditions
3	50/50 odds of occurrence
4	>50% odds of occurrence
5	Very likely to occur

The method's name comes from the Greek fable about Cassandra, who had the gift of foresight but the curse that others could not understand about her prophecy or warnings. Behind the scoring is a weighted calculation of social goodwill, the readiness of a rapid response team, an inventory of the issues facing a brand, and the relative risk those issues present.

Similar approaches exist. The Coast Guard, for example, uses one called the Surface Operations Risk Calculation Worksheet.[20]

During my years at Motorola, I learned about risk calculation inside the Six Sigma method.

For twenty-five years, I served as the senior communication leader for the Austin Marathon—a 26.2-mile endurance event with an average annual participation of about 15,000 runners. Endurance races aren't just athletic challenges; they're logistical and safety minefields. I have known many race directors over the years and have consulted with several other endurance events. For most, I've used the Cassandra Calculator to help assess the likelihood and severity of something going wrong. Here is a snapshot of a completed exercise for a marathon event:

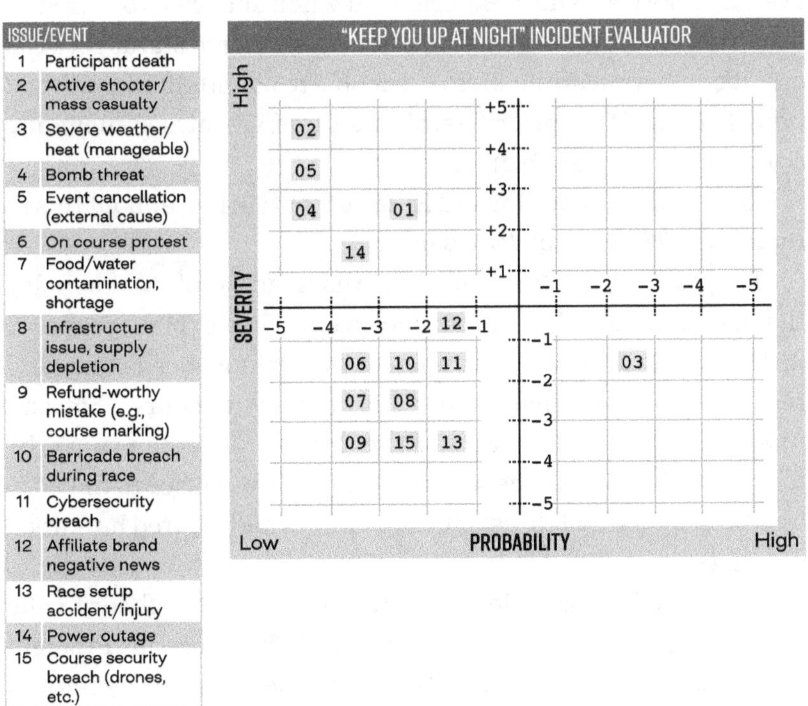

As you can see, on the X-axis, we assessed the likelihood of an event occurring, while on the Y-axis, we made a guess at how bad the damage would be if the event occurred. A participant death (#1), for example, sits in the high-severity, low-probability quadrant. Runner fatalities, usually due to undiagnosed medical conditions, occur about one out of every 100,000 opportunities. While that's seldom, I can attest firsthand that they happen.

What's interesting about endurance events is that bad weather (#3) is the only high-probability event. Often, organizations will focus their efforts on preparing for bad weather, because it is the most foreseeable issue. However, they cannot prepare for other crises that can occur.

Why are so many organizations often underprepared for these events? Like Cassandra experienced when she tried to warn the leaders of Troy not to bring a giant wooden horse statue into the city, it's sometimes difficult to get people to pay attention until bad news breaks. Other priorities, distractions, and biases, including optimism bias, are to blame.[21]

Robert Meyer and Howard Kunreuther talk more about this in their book *The Ostrich Paradox*.

They identify six types of biases that lead people to downplay the likelihood of crisis events occurring. They explain that optimism bias is an "It won't happen to me" mindset. The bias gets recalibrated every time a new thing happens, of course. You can imagine how the organizers of the Boston Marathon think differently today about race security than they did prior to the 2013 bombing that killed three of their runners and injured hundreds of others.[22]

Nassim Nicholas Taleb, inventor of Black Swan theory, calls optimism bias, "The Lucretius Problem." The Lucretius Problem is a cognitive bias where people assume the worst-case scenario they have experienced is the worst likely scenario, failing to grasp that a worse event could still occur. The Lucretius Problem highlights our difficulty in grasping the potential for unprecedented events. We underestimate the possibility of events outside our experience, which leads to inadequate preparation for extreme scenarios.[23]

Lucretius's problems have a home in Chandler's Crisis Stages model. They make themselves visible where the shaded areas overlap. These overlaps highlight the places where pressure is created, and pressure, as Amazon CEO Jeff Bezos made famous, is a "complexifier" that warps clarity and sound decision-making.[24]

Emergency responders begin the Response stage from an incident-management standpoint when they are activated and rolling to a scene. From a communications standpoint, however, it begins when a rapid response team is activated.

In the Management stage of a crisis's life cycle, you share critical information with stakeholders, especially those impacted by the incident. Conditions may change quickly during this period, and it's crucial to understand the physical and mental states of those involved, those impacted, and those actively standing by to get involved either in person or on social media.

During the Resolution stage of a crisis, the transition to recovery gets underway and corrective action begins. Resolution differs from recovery. In resolution, people fix broken things, or someone promises to fix something; recovery is one thing, but reputation—trust in a brand—must be restored. The former is a function of managerial administration; the latter lies within the province of leadership.

Chandler's model sets the context for understanding how a brand can navigate through a bad-news break. But how? What are the steps? I'll ask this question again in the next chapter.

Before we get to that, a warning. This hat, which sits on a shelf in my office, is a gift from my friend and colleague Russ Rhea. It's a tribute to the 1970s band Foghat, and it's also a reminder that crisis events can put even an experienced decision-maker's head in an emotion-filled fog.

In high-pressure situations, we feel pressure to diagnose and prescribe a path through Chandler's model, much like a doctor prescribes a course of treatment for a patient. The fog, however, makes this very difficult.

By the way, a doctor—an oncologist, to be precise—provided significant inspiration for this book. Modern theory of how to break bad news originated in medicine. In 1847, the American Medical Association's original code of ethics stated that doctors should not "make gloomy prognostications." Instead, they were advised to be "ministers of hope and comfort," fearing that giving a patient bad news could damage them or even drive them to suicide. This guideline prevailed in the profession for more than a century. As recently as 1951, the *Journal of the American Medical Association* (JAMA) published an article suggesting ways for doctors to deceive patients and their families about their cancer diagnoses. "Call cancer an ulcer or infection," JAMA advised. The same article recommended lobotomies for patients who reacted badly.[25]

Dr. Robert Buckman—a British oncologist whose career

included performing in Cambridge University's Footlights Revue in the early 1970s with John Cleese of *Monty Python's Flying Circus* fame—had a better idea.[26] After becoming a patient—he suffered from a congenital muscle disease that almost killed him—Buckman noticed how awful his doctors were at explaining his condition to him. His experience, personality, and training prompted him to design SPIKES, a method for breaking bad news to patients.

SPIKES is an acronym for "Setting Up, Perception, Invitation, Knowledge, Emotions, and Strategy and Summary." Buckman explained, "Your ability to empathize with the patient's emotions is the single most important characteristic of good and supportive news breaking. Without it, you're going to appear insensitive and of little support."[27] Physicians around the world still use SPIKES today, and it may be another tool for you to adapt to your own purposes.

Buckman's breakthrough thinking sets the stage for the rest of this book in three ways:

1. First, he reminds us that breaking bad news is emotional. In Buckman's experience, breaking bad news is stressful when the deliverer of the bad news is inexperienced or there are limited prospects for successful treatment.[28]
2. Second, breaking bad news is inevitable. At some point, a brand is going to find itself in trouble. It is an inevitable event in any executive's career, just as an oncologist must inevitably tell a patient they have cancer.
3. Finally, Buckman demonstrated through SPIKES that a model could synthesize the method of breaking bad news. This is worth appreciating: Gut-wrenching, fog-inducing, emotionally jarring, life-changing information can be delivered through a learnable, repeatable, and predictive model.

That breakthrough notion sets the stage for what comes next.

CHAPTER 2

MODELS, MUNGER, AND MORE

"If the spaghetti hits the fan, we're really in trouble."

—General Buck Turgidson

Robert Buckman's comedy career may not have brought him the fame of comedians like John Cleese or Eric Idle, but if Buckman had met Charlie Munger, it may have been a newsworthy occasion.

Charlie Munger was the visionary financial partner of Warren Buffett for forty-five years prior to Munger's death in 2023. They met when they were both young men and, together, they created Berkshire Hathaway Inc., the most successful holding company in history. Buffett has often stated he would have been far less successful without Charlie Munger's influence. For Munger's part, he unequivocally attributes both men's successes largely to the use of mental models.

The philosopher Alfred Korzybski talked about models in a paper he delivered at a meeting of the American Association for the Advancement of Science in New Orleans, Louisiana, on December 28, 1931: "A map is not the territory it represents, but if correct, it has a similar structure to the territory, which accounts for its usefulness."[29]

A map is an abstraction derived from something that is not the thing itself. Korzybski, it seems, believed that many people confuse models of reality with reality itself.

In his book *Charlie Munger: The Complete Investor*, author Tren Griffin explains Munger's notion of "elementary, worldly wisdom"—a set of interdisciplinary mental models involving economics, business, psychology, ethics, and management—and how drawing on them "helps one keep the emotions out of decision-making and avoid the pitfalls of bad judgment."[30]

Munger advocates using mental models as filters to help choose which options to focus on and which to ignore. Combined with your intuition and based on your understanding of the world, they can remove blind spots and help you plan better solutions. Models simplify the complex and, as a result, reduce uncertainty. This is especially important as behavioral science teaches that biases affect decision-making, especially under pressure. Using mental models makes us aware of our biases while improving our conclusions.

Scores of mental models exist. For a wonderful exploration, *The Decision Book* by Mikael Krogerus and Roman Tschäppeler is a must-read. It's packed with easy-to-understand models, reinforcing Munger's argument that mastering a handful can provide a better understanding of how the world works. As Munger said, "80 or 90 important models will carry about 90 percent of the freight in making you a worldly-wise person. And of those, only a mere handful really carry very heavy freight."[31]

Munger has an important caveat to the subject of models. He says, "What are the models? Well, the first rule is that you've got to have multiple models—because if you just have one or two that you're using, the nature of human psychology is such that you'll torture reality so that it fits your models, or at least you'll think it does. You become the equivalent of a chiropractor who, of course, is the great boob in medicine... You've got to have models in your head," he says, "you've got to array your experience—both vicarious and direct—on this latticework of models."[32]

A latticework, with the models serving as the tools, is what I think of as the toolbox created in this book. Together they (a) help anyone in a brand crisis make better sense of the world through a system capable of diagnosing complex communication challenges and (b) provide a method for prescribing a smart course of action using a single, latticed communication model to guide decision-making in the fog. To a great extent, the toolbox equips you to become a choice architect—one who "has responsibility for organizing the context in which people make decisions."[33]

The Rapid Response Model you'll find in the next chapter is yet another tool. Like the crow's nest on a ship, think of it as seeing what's coming in a fast-moving situation inside of Chandler's high-level map. Like Munger instructs, it's a compass made from several smart thinkers in multiple disciplines showing the way forward through the foggy situations the rapid response teams have to navigate through to be successful.

How about a quick anecdote about a foggy situation? Here's how it goes:

A student went to visit a professor at the professor's home. A dog was playing outside the house in the yard. When the professor opened the door to let the student in, the dog ran into the house. Some hours later, after they had finished their conversation, the professor asked the student, "Do you always travel with your dog?" The student replied, "It's not my dog. I thought it was yours."[34]

Pause for a moment and reflect on the scene described above. What assumptions did someone make? Were they right? If not, you get a sense of what fog does. It creates assumptions that drive suboptimal decision-making or worse.

Television shows like *Scandal* or movies like *Wolfs* have never helped. They fog executives' brains with the idea that a "fixer" is all you need to make things better. For brands that don't employ covert operations teams that make people and problems disappear, it's best to characterize fixers as fictional.

Credible crisis communications professionals would never claim to be fixers—we're much more like very good navigators and models make that navigation possible. Models can improve the ability to both diagnose and prescribe smart courses of action, even in the most challenging communication circumstances. As Krogerus and Tschäppeler put it, "When we encounter chaos, we seek ways to structure it, to see through it, or at least gain an overview of it. Models help us reduce the complexity of a situation by enabling us to dismiss most of it and concentrate on what is important."[35]

Unfortunately, there is a trick to all of this. Like any tools, to wield models for greatest effect, you must study them and practice using them. As Munger put it, "You've got to have models in your head. And you've got to array your experience—both vicarious and direct—on this latticework of models."[36]

Here's where we run into a challenge. As mentioned earlier in the book, by nature, crises are low-frequency events. Nassim Nicholas Taleb labels them "Black Swan" events and adds low predictability, high impact, and the human tendency to discount their probability into the mix.[37] Unless you make your living as a crisis consultant, you rarely have an opportunity to use the tools necessary to navigate a bad-news break. Why is that a problem? Supreme Court Justice Oliver Wendell Holmes Jr. once said, "Most people think dramatically, not quantitatively," and that is especially true in ambiguous, shifting, uncertain situations.[38]

In *Glass Jaw*, author and crisis expert Eric Dezenhall explains it better. When an investigative reporter asked him why corporations are so bad at defending their reputations during controversies, Dezenhall replied, "It's not what they do. Companies make and sell stuff. They don't fight critics for a living. And they dread the very idea of a fight."[39]

We need models, especially in the midst of unfamiliar, perhaps chaotic situations. This means to be valuable, any tool intended to be employed in reputation management must be easy to use. If it's too complicated, we won't understand it enough to put it to use in the fog of an incident. Along with ease of use, models and tools are well-suited for the work when they have these characteristics:

1. They make the complex simple and create the opportunity for insight. They may not represent reality, but they are proxies for reality.
2. They produce meaningful explanations and predictions of likely future consequences where the cost of being wrong is high.[40]
3. They are more reliable with repetition.
4. They are not processes, although some of the best models and tools contain sequences.
5. As with so many things in life, a tool's effectiveness depends on the user, which has more to do with the willingness to invest time to master its potential.

The tools presented in this book work for a variety of reasons and in a variety of ways. To assemble a latticework of them helpful for crisis-related decision-making, it's useful to look at a few.

Here, for starters, is Joseph Voros's Futures Cone. This tool provides a framework that helps us think strategically about the many ways the future could unfold. As Voros explains, "The seven types of alternative future...are all considered to be subjective judgments about ideas about the future that are based in the present moment."[41]

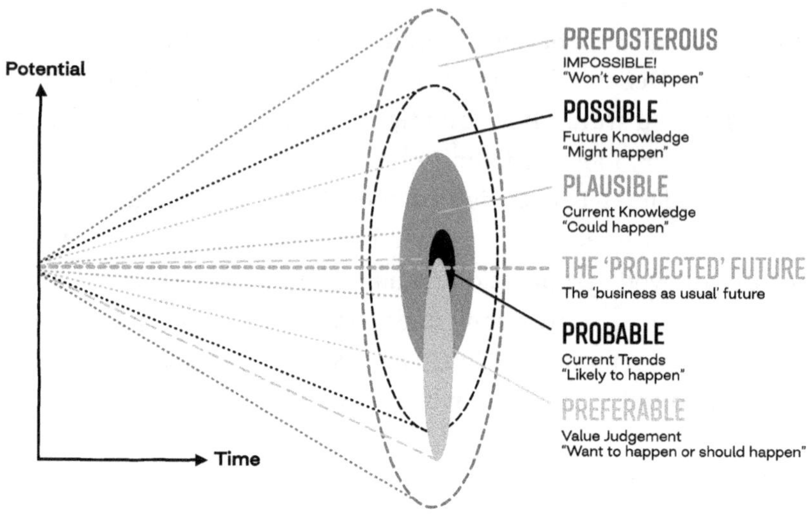

Too often, organizations plan only for the most obvious projected outcomes. This narrow thinking leaves them vulnerable to disruptions that lie outside conventional expectations. Voros's Cone serves as a reminder that the future rarely follows a predictable path. By considering a broader array of potential outcomes—including those that seem unlikely—organizations can develop strategies that are more resilient, adaptive, and prepared for the unexpected.

Next, let's look at Leon Festinger's Cognitive Dissonance Framework, published in 1975.

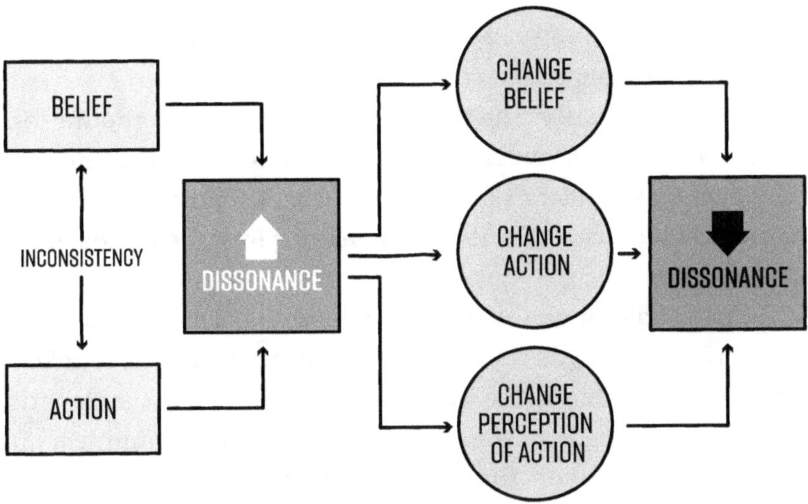

Festinger's simple, yet powerful, framework explains the psychological phenomenon of "cognitive dissonance," a state of significant mental discomfort when our actions contradict our beliefs.[42]

Festinger's model, an important diagnostic device to throw in your toolbox, has significant implications for reputation managers. First, dissonance is an emotional state.[43] Reputation managers have to make decisions under emotional pressure when the weather fronts depicted in Chandler's Map collide. Second, Festinger's theory suggests we have an inner drive to hold our attitudes and behaviors in harmony (cognitive consistency), and avoid disharmony.[44] Finally, when an inconsistency between attitudes or behaviors (dissonance) exists, something must change to eliminate the dissonance. What do we do to resolve dissonance when it occurs? Just about anything.

In crisis situations, executives might prefer self-justification to admitting mistakes and asking for forgiveness.[45] Why? Because our emotions harmonize in the absence of cognitive dissonance. It makes us feel better when we can rationalize away a bad situation. When our actions and behaviors are out of sync, however, "The drive to be perceived as consistent constitutes a highly potent weapon of influence."[46]

This is especially true if a brand experiencing a reputation crisis has made its values and beliefs public in prior communications to stakeholders. Echoing Bill Coletti's definition, the brand has put expectations for its own behavior into the minds of its stakeholders.

Robert Cialdini, one of the great modern scholars of persuasion, says, "If I can get you to make a commitment (that is, to take a stand, to go on record), I will have set the stage for your automatic and ill-considered consistency with that earlier commitment. Once a stand is taken, there is a natural tendency to behave in ways that are stubbornly consistent with the stand."[47]

Take the case of Chipotle Mexican Grill.

Over several years, the brand suffered through persistent foodborne illness incidents. The reason the brand received so much attention from stakeholders, the media, and the public is the contrast created by its public commitments to freshness versus multiple incidents of customers contracting food poisoning. Through all those events, the brand only slightly changed its messaging. Does that seem strange? Not when viewed through Festinger's lens. It's likely that Chipotle weighed the dissonance it experienced because of foodborne illness incidents against the dissonance it might experience by publicly revising its unshakable devotion to freshness.

You'll read more about Chipotle later, but for the moment, a Ralph Waldo Emerson quote feels appropriate. He said, "A foolish consistency is the hobgoblin of little minds, adored by little statesmen and philosophers and divines."[48] Emerson tells us that when we do the same things over and over but expect different outcomes, we're nuts, and yet, dissonance makes it terribly difficult to break free from hard-anchored positions.

It's good to understand cognitive dissonance and the remarkable power it has over people's minds. In crisis events, it is the psychological precursor to pressure, and pressure has a profound impact on decision-making.

This leaves us on the doorstep of answers to our main question: How can a brand navigate through a bad-news break? What are the steps? My response is forthcoming. I'll set it up by stating five core guiding principles:

1. Reputation is based on the expectation of what an organization will do next, which is based on the public's perception of what a brand has done or said repeatedly. This sets the baseline for "normal" inside an organization and outside to stakeholders.
2. Models, figures, widgets, diagrams, templates, and frameworks are useful tools for understanding life and solving problems. They help keep the emotions out of decision-making and avoid the pitfalls of bad judgment. As Warren Buffett said, "Risk comes from not knowing what you're doing."[49] Suitable tools address this by simplifying the complex and reducing uncertainty.
3. When bad news breaks, like weather fronts colliding, the pressure is on. This creates dissonance. Something unexpected, unwelcome, disruptive, costly, and reputation-scarring has developed, and whatever the bad thing is, it's public information. The brand's stated values, attitudes, and beliefs clash with exposed behaviors or actions.
4. The speed with which social and traditional media race to report news combines to pressurize crisis situations.
5. Dissonance creates an overwhelming desire to restore harmony. Restoring internal normalcy and external expectations isn't just a wish; it is an emotional tidal wave caused by inconsistency between beliefs and behaviors.

Here's one of the dumbest quotes ever delivered by an executive in a crisis, proving the existence of dissonance and the drive to restore normalcy:

"We're sorry for the massive disruption it's caused their lives. There's no one who wants this over more than I do. I'd like my life back."[50]

These are the words of then-BP Energy CEO Tony Hayward in the aftermath of the 2010 Deepwater Horizon explosion and oil spill in the Gulf of Mexico. Eleven people died, and seventeen were injured.

About 210 million gallons of oil and 1.8 million gallons of chemical dispersants spilled into the gulf, polluting the coast and the seafloor. The environmental disaster devastated the US, and Hayward's only offer was, "I'd like my life back."[51] The quote is proof of how the drive to reduce dissonance makes even very smart people do and say just about anything.

Every brand is likely to experience a crisis at some point. Unlike opportunities, they are emotion-driven, pressure-packed situations catalyzed by dissonance. To manage them well, we need a latticework of models—a collection of tools—to help us get through the tough decision-making ahead.

Agreed? If so, we're ready to move forward.

CHAPTER 3

RAPID RESPONSE MODEL

"Let our advance worrying become advance thinking and planning."
—WINSTON CHURCHILL

Nearly every client I have had the privilege of serving has experienced a reputation-damaging incident. Because we are interested in the energy, food, and health sectors, crisis events are not unusual.

In the food business, for example, a recall, withdrawal, or safety alert occurs in the US almost every day.[52] Imagine if we were talking about oil spills, plane crashes, or electric-grid blackouts!

Food recalls can bankrupt a business. Depending on severity, a recall may disrupt operations, require a sudden cash outlay to pay for reverse logistics and shipping, and require years to restore reputation. A joint study by the Food Marketing Institute and the Grocery Manufacturers Association (GMA) estimated the average food recall cost companies $10 million in direct costs, a number that doesn't take potential litigation into account.[53] In a companion survey, GMA found that 5 percent of food companies incurred over $100 million in direct and indirect costs associated with recall events.[54]

Where do these indirect costs come from? Lost trust is one source. In a Harris Interactive poll, 55 percent of consumers said they would switch brands following a recall, 15 percent said they would never buy the brand again, and 21 percent said they would avoid purchasing any brand made by the manufacturer of the recalled product.[55]

Unchecked outrage is another source. Remember "pink slime"?

In June 2017, Disney, the parent company of ABC News, settled a defamation lawsuit brought against it by Beef Products Incorporated (BPI) for a reported $177 million. BPI sued ABC for $1.9 billion over a series of news reports broadcast on *ABC World News* with Diane Sawyer regarding the company's production of lean, finely textured beef (LFTB), a beef product created by placing small pieces of lean meat in a centrifuge to produce a bulk product. The meat is treated with a small amount of ammonium hydroxide, an antimicrobial agent composed of water and ammonia mixed together.

In 2012, ABC News correspondent Jim Avila referred to the product on-air as "pink slime." The network used the phrase over 350 times in subsequent broadcasts. During the trial, BPI lawyer Dan Webb described the swift, extreme harm ABC's reports had caused his client, saying BPI "took about thirty years to succeed, and it took ABC less than 30 days to severely damage the company."[56]

Avila didn't coin the term that caused BPI so much harm. In a December 2009 piece, *New York Times* reporter Michael Moss wrote, "Another US Department of Agriculture microbiologist, Gerald Zirnstein, called the processed beef 'pink slime' in a 2002 email message to colleagues and said, 'I do not consider the stuff to be ground beef, and I consider allowing it in ground beef to be a form of fraudulent labeling.'"[57]

BPI eventually settled its suit with ABC News for a reported $177 million, but more cash was likely involved.[58] *Fortune* magazine and other news outlets reported insurance companies paid

BPI roughly $50 million, although one insurer, AIG, sued Disney to avoid paying $25 million of its portion of the bill.[59]

The pink slime case reminds us just how quickly consumer sentiment can shift and wreak havoc on a brand. Even though a vast amount of scientific evidence confirmed LFTB was beef, and the ammonium hydroxide it contained is present in many common foods, such as chocolate and cheese, consumers found the product disgusting and were appalled that it was being served to children in schools.

Did the industry miss an opportunity to do a better job of branding LFTB? Absolutely. We can't un-ring that bell, but we can learn a couple important lessons from the case:

1. A March 2015 *National Geographic* magazine feature entitled "Why Do Many Reasonable People Doubt Science?" explored the general public's attitudes about proven scientific knowledge on subjects ranging from fluoridation to climate change. Here's a great line from the article: "The world crackles with real and imaginary hazards and distinguishing the former from the latter isn't easy."[60]

2. All the scientists in the world couldn't turn back consumer nausea generated by the phrase "pink slime." Gone are the days when a small circle of experts—academics, scientists, and even authors affiliated with reputable news outlets—could single-handedly influence public opinion. The internet has democratized information and made it possible to live in a bubble that lets in only information supporting an existing point of view, isolating readers and viewers from divergent perspectives and even scientific facts.

This is especially true in the wake of the COVID-19 pandemic. Trust in experts, including scientists, has eroded over time. According to the Pew Center, "Overall, 57% of Americans say science has had a mostly positive effect on society. This share is down 8 percentage points since November 2021 and down 16 points since before the start of the coronavirus outbreak."[61] The Pew study cites political polarization as a major driver of distrust. Years ago, Tim Berners-Lee, the inventor of the internet, was prescient in his misgivings about how the web might accelerate the disintegration of trust. He asked:

> Will the net lead to a monolithic (American) culture, or will it foster even more disparate interest groups than exist today? Will it enable a true democracy by informing the voting public of the realities behind state decisions, or in practice will it harbor ghettos of bigotry where emotional intensity rather than truth gains the readership? It is for us to decide, but it is not trivial to assess the impact of simple engineering decisions on the answers to such questions.[62]

3. Consumers demand more transparency about the food they eat and the products they use. As transparent as BPI may have been about LFTB, it didn't explain in a reassuring manner how the product was made. Further, it's difficult to find content touting the nutritional benefits and value of LFTB. Thus, the prevailing attitude about it made any defense of LFTB pretty tough.

4. Along with the MAHA Movement (Make America Healthy Again), a host of unflattering, Netflix-accessible documentaries about food—*King Corn, The Magic Pill, Food Choices*, and *Cowspiracy*, to name a few—make it clear that food producers, in particular, must respond more swiftly to any incident threatening to damage their brands.

All of this means that brands have a real challenge on their hands. When a consumer herd begins a stampede, how can reputation managers quickly and effectively respond? My response is: "Turn the herd."

Like cowboys who ride to the front of a stampede and nudge the lead steer in a new direction, the Rapid Response Model diagram shown below helps you see what is ahead so you can steer a crisis event in a better direction. The tool leans heavily on Festinger's cognitive dissonance theory. As you dive into it, I encourage you to score it against the principles of a good model presented in the previous chapter. If it passes your test, you'll likely want to keep it close from here on out.

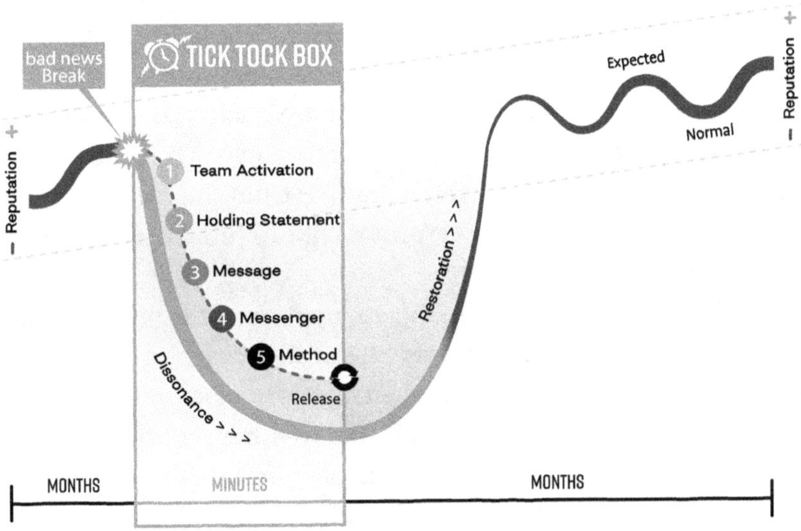

REPUTATION MODULATION AND THE NORMAL/EXPECTED ZONE

Do you recall the discussion earlier regarding dissonance and the pressure and fog it creates? When bad news breaks, stakeholders and reputation managers are driven to reduce the dissonance. Their goal is to return to a state of emotional harmony where attitudes and beliefs match behaviors and actions. What does that mean? It requires realigning with the expectations of stakeholders and feels like what "normal" ought to feel like.

A tornado flattened a large part of our family farm in northeast Iowa on the afternoon of November 9, 1975. The tornado destroyed our barn, a repurposed aircraft hangar, and everything it housed. Four brick grain silos, three Butler grain bins, four outbuildings, tractors, farm implements, a dozen stacks of silage, and about sixty head of Holstein cattle were all scattered to the wind. Even the motorhome, which a family friend had parked at our farm, was toppled over and blew across the front yard.

My family and I rode out the storm in our cellar, listening to the locomotive sound of the wind churning above. Within only a few minutes, stone-cold silence set in. We made our way outside to see an eerie sky—a peculiar blend of greenish-yellow and gray-black roiling clouds. The wreckage of almost everything we owned surrounded us. Somehow, a few of my 4-H Club chickens survived. Those silly birds were clucking around like nothing had happened. It was pretty surreal.

In the archives of KWWL-TV is a mention of the weather that day noting that at the time, it was "the third-largest November tornado outbreak in Iowa history...when nine tornadoes touched down across the state."[63] We lived inside that weather report. Our place was destroyed and with it, the dream of operating a family farm.

Had my parents been cold, detached business people, they would have just packed us up, and we would have made a *Grapes of Wrath*-style escape to somewhere else. Instead, the drive for normalcy kicked in. Over the next several weeks, heavy equipment operators excavated an enormous hole in the field a few yards from our house.

Over the subsequent weeks, we shoveled, tossed, and dumped all the remains of our blasted-to-pieces farm into that pit—every splintered piece of lumber, every busted brick, every bit of wasted silage, every animal carcass, every piece of debris within a mile radius. Aside from what the scrap metal salvagers came and took, it all got dropped into that hole and covered up. Then we went back to school and to work; back to "normal."

I sometimes wonder if any family ever gets back to normal after that kind of trauma. Likely not, but without veering into a therapy discussion, what I can attest to is how our psyches are hard-wired to seek normalcy.

When you're on the inside of a brand, "normal" is an appealing emotional state. The same is true for the minds of stakeholders. They may be external to a brand—a consumer, a supplier, or an influencer—but they too are consistency seekers. Their type of consistency is called an expectation.

Scholars in crisis communications have studied this notion. Siomkos and Kurzbard, for example, found consumer responses to bad-news breaks are based on factors such as the company's reputation and their prior expectations about a brand.[64] As you'll read later in the Blue Bell Creameries crisis, a brand's personality can also make a difference, as well as the level of commitment a consumer has toward a brand.[65] Likewise, scholars have studied the relationship between an organization and its public. Meeting expectations is "integral in situations where the relationship is put under strain, such as in crisis situations."[66]

It's fair to say that a reputation comprises an uncountable number of impressions accumulated in the minds of people around you/your brand (also known as your stakeholders) to form a shared expectation. When the twin ideas of normal and expected form up, they create a standard against which a brand is judged, especially during a crisis. The standard contains value judgments of both what has been and what should be.

Around the Rapid Response Model, the zone extending left to right across the diagram represents the preferred—the normal (internally) and expected (externally)—trajectory of a brand's reputation. Within the boundaries of the positive and negative poles, you see a sine wave, which represents the everyday ups and downs every brand experiences. At a meta level, we call this "life."

THE REPUTATION MODULATION SINE WAVE

Ever heard of the "Food Babe"? She is Vani Hari, an online influencer who AI search engines say has nearly 2.4 million followers. Her disciples regard her as an evangelist of sorts, because since 2011, she has devoted her life to criticizing the food industry. Once upon a time, Hari ate a lot of junk food, which—no surprise—eventually landed her in the hospital. During her recovery, she resolved to start eating better and living a healthy life. Her testimonial reads as follows: "I didn't go to nutrition school to learn this. I had to teach myself everything, spending thousands of hours researching and talking to experts. As I began to learn more, I was no longer duped by big business marketing tactics or confused by lengthy food labels, and it became easier for me to live in this over-processed world. Most importantly, the more I learned and the more lessons I put into action, the better I felt and wanted to tell everyone about it!"[67]

Today, if Food Babe posts negative commentary about your product, you're going to have a bad day, and the boring, low-trust scientists or industry experts you may enlist to counter her opinion are going to have a tough time changing the minds of her disciples. From a reputation modulation standpoint, you're going to find yourself in a trough.

A negative comment by Hari may drive sentiment about your brand one day, but something good may happen the next. A positive financial report or a cool new product announcement can push a reputation back into a positive peak. These reputation-making ebbs and flows can be measured by any number of social-listening and media-monitoring tools. The sine wave of reputation moves up or down over time, forming an external expectation of how a brand comports itself, what it stands for, and how it should behave in the future, along with an internal sense of normal.

An example of how the reputation modulation sine wave moves up with positive news can be found in the case of Impossible Foods, makers of plant-based meat, which rivals organic ground beef in terms of taste, nutrition, and versatility. When it first debuted, Impossible Foods won awards at the Consumer Electronics Show (CES), including the "Most Unexpected Product," "Most Impactful Product," and "Best of the Best." It was the first food ever show-cased at the tech show, which for decades has been the global stage where next-generation technology innovations have been introduced in the marketplace. The company's food chemistry developments using heme, the molecule responsible for the flavors resulting when meat is cooked, was considered a technology breakthrough.[68]

Buzz about Impossible Foods was hard to overlook. Molly Wood, then host of the radio show *MarketPlace Tech*, ran a story shortly after CES with the headline, "Investors are Hungry for Meat-Replacement Technologies," which made the point that at the time, Impossible Foods was enjoying time at the top of the sine wave zone, and it was joined there by rival Beyond Meat. After going public, Beyond Meat's market cap increased to more than $13 billion.[69]

It may be fun to be at the top of the sine wave zone but the old saying "what goes up must come down" remains as true as ever. The sine wave flows inside a zone and a scale depicted in months. It takes many, many months for a brand to build a reputation, and no matter how good that reputation, the inevitable negative trough is going to come, and for both brands, that has been true.

A 2025 CNBC profile of the plant-based meat replacement industry bashed both brands. Consumer uptake of the products has waned, and Beyond's stock price has fallen over 90 percent since the beginning of the hype cycle. High cost, bland restaurant partnership results, taste, and even "better-for-you" ultra-processed food confusion have all complicated the reputations of the brands.[70]

It may not be fun for Impossible and Beyond to bump along the negative rail of the zone, but as long as they stay inside the normal-expected zone, the overall reputation of the brands can continue their up-and-to-the-right trajectory. Both remind us that people build reputations, and they build them over time.

CHAPTER 4

TWO RAPID RESPONSE TEAM TOOLS

"Never awake me when you have good news to announce, because with good news nothing presses; but when you have bad news, arouse me immediately, for then there is not an instant to be lost."

—NAPOLEON BONAPARTE

In *The Cat in the Hat,* Dr. Seuss introduced the twins, Thing One and Thing Two. They were, to put it mildly, troublemakers. I have omitted two things from the Rapid Response Model diagram but like Thing One and Thing Two, they will cause your brand serious trouble if you are unaware of them, so let's attend to them at this point before moving deeper into the model.

Remember Korzybski's statement, "A map is not the territory it represents…"? By design, models leave elements of the territory out. Think about a recipe (which is a model of sorts) in a cookbook. What is an enormous omission in every cookbook? It is assumed you have a kitchen, appliances, pots, pans, and all the gadgets necessary to produce the dish in the picture.

The same is true for the Rapid Response Model. It omits the work necessary to assemble a team of people responsible for responding to bad-news incidents before one occurs. With my clients, I use the term "rapid response team" (RRT) when referring to this assumed-to-exist group.

THE RAPID RESPONSE TEAM MATRIX

Other experts have written about the same subject. Bill Coletti calls for the formation of a reputation management council.[71] James Haggerty believes in establishing a chief crisis officer and a core team.[72] Eric Dezenhall likes the idea of a less-formal structure. He writes, "The best clients are large corporations or institutions that have endured controversy before and have a strong, small, and improvisational leadership team directly engaged in the crisis at hand..."[73] Peter Stanton also advocates for a core team and has written, "Core team planning focuses on procedures for making decisions under pressure but in a disciplined and thoughtful fashion."[74]

Richard Levick and Larry Smith put more into this subject when they wrote about the idea of a crisis committee in their book *Stop the Presses*.[75] They outlined the general structure of a rapid response team by identifying key roles: a decision-maker, either the CEO or a person designated to act on the CEO's behalf; the head of corporate communications; law department representatives; C-suite executives; technical specialists or content experts; and outside PR counsel. It was good work, but more is needed.

I'll be more prescriptive than these authors, as well as a little counterintuitive in designing my ideal rapid response team in the table that follows. The matrix is another tool you can put in your toolbox.

RAPID RESPONSE TEAM MATRIX

TEAM MEMBER	RESPONSIBILITIES	NOTES
Rapid Response Team Coordinator (RRTC)	Sets up the RRT's convening capabilities: designated conference rooms at key locations, a secure conference call phone bridge, and virtual meeting tools to securely connect the team and manage group work product creation. Once approved by the chief decision-maker (CDM—see below), the RRTC activates the RRT using a multichannel (email, text, phone) utility, such as AlertMedia or any number of similar group notification methods. Opens the online collaboration bridge (e.g., Teams or Zoom) and takes roll. Contacts backup experts to fill in for missing team members. Drafts statements in real time for immediate approval. Tracks action items. Drafts the team's after-action report. Activates a deputy RRT coordinator to assist, if needed.	My "counterintuitive" remark above applies to this position. In my experience, the effectiveness of a rapid response team rises and falls not on the chief decision-maker, but on this role. The RRTC's pre-crisis work ensures the RRT can activate efficiently. In my experience, this is the piece most often missing from a brand's response preparation. During a crisis, the RRTC's ability to draft statements, talking points, and other support materials, while maintaining version control, is essential, so choose this person wisely. Look for characteristics that include both the ability to see a big picture and a healthy obsession with details and precision.
Chief Decision-Maker (CDM)	Approves rapid response team activation. Assesses incident impact. Manages RRT processing. Shuts down unproductive dialogue. Advises on outbound communication. Approves official outbound communication. Informs executives and important stakeholders on a prioritized basis.	The CDM is an executive who, by title or appointment, heads the RRT. This doesn't necessarily mean the CEO or similarly titled person by default, but it means someone who has the authority and influence to decide how to respond to an incident and activate resources 24/7/365.

TEAM MEMBER	RESPONSIBILITIES	NOTES
Deputy Chief Decision-Maker (DCDM)	Confers with CDM to determine if RRT activation is necessary. Assesses incident impact. Advises on outbound communication. In the absence of the CDM, manages the RRT. Approves official outbound communication in the absence of the CDM. Musters subject-matter experts, as needed.	RRTs should have a strong #2 decision-maker ready to take the lead if the CDM is unavailable, and Murphy's Law warns that virtually every crisis incident will happen while the CDM is on a plane, out of the country, under anesthesia, or out of contact for some other reason. Likewise, your mother was right: Nothing good ever happens after midnight, which seems to be when most bad news breaks. The DCDM must be able to operate in the fog at the least convenient times.
Senior Communication Leader (SCL)	Assesses incident impact on multiple stakeholders, especially internal. Directs development of official outbound communication. Activates outside PR agency for support. Preps incident spokesperson.	During a crisis event, it's crucial for the SCL to accurately predict how stakeholders may interpret external stakeholder expectations. The essential responsibility the SCL plays before a bad-news break is leading a brand's issues forecasting team using tools like our Cassandra Calculator™ and guiding the development of a rapid response plan.
Communication Manager (CM)	Assesses potential media interest. Activates tracking of social media and broadcast media. Finalizes outbound communication in real time for immediate approval. Coordinates outbound communication distribution through earned, social, and owned channels. Serves as initial incident spokesperson, if appropriate.	I advise clients to allow the person in this role to serve as the initial spokesperson for two reasons: to issue the holding statement and to shield the CDM and key leaders from a barrage of inbound questions. The CDM must focus on the incident at hand and can always be called on later to speak on the brand's behalf, if necessary.

TEAM MEMBER	RESPONSIBILITIES	NOTES
Legal Counsel (LC)	Assesses and communicates liability risks. Relays regulatory requirements. Advises on outbound communication.	Legal counsel is crucial to an effective RRT, but they have to know their role. Legal counsel advises on risk and liability but should not be in the business of wordsmithing statements to death. Time is of the essence, so war room arguments due to law department preferences that are stylistic, not substantive, aren't useful. Haggerty devotes a few pages to the role lawyers play on an RRT and reminds us: Lawyers are trained to compete, even with others on the same team. Lawyering is an adversarial profession by nature. Lawyers use argument to explore issues and arrive at conclusions logically, not emotionally. Lawyers look for precedent; they use indoctrination thinking vs. creative problem-solving.[76] For communications people and even decision-makers, these traits can be vexing, but no RRT is complete without qualified legal counsel.
Subject-Matter Experts (SMEs)	Assesses incident impact on customers, consumers, suppliers, facility, financial, IT, marketing, security, or human resources. Supports CDM and DCDM decisions by activating staff and serving as information gatherers, reporters, and fact providers. Opens channels of communication to outside experts and services, as needed.	These can be executives representing key functions, including food safety, supply chain management, and customer relations. Given the situation, CFOs, CIOs, CMOs, CHROs, facility directors, or executive admins can also be SMEs. Add as many SMEs to the RRT as needed. If they can help provide or organize relevant information in the midst of a dynamic situation, they're valuable.

Why haven't I included the formation and training of a rapid response team in the Rapid Response Model? That tool is focused on the fast-moving action of navigating through a bad-news break, leaving deliberate, disciplined work like RRT training to be represented in the reputation modulation sine wave leading up to a spaghetti-hits-the-fan moment. A well-designed and trained RRT takes time—years, in fact—to be fully prepared to take on a reputation challenge.

THE RAPID RESPONSE TEAM PLAN

Mike Tyson, the world champion boxer, once said, "Everyone has a plan until they get punched in the mouth."[77] I love that quote, and we all ought to pay attention to it. For decades, brands have spent untold sums of money creating three-ring binders filled with everything a team needs to know to manage a crisis. The value of crisis plans like these is reflected in the cost of the paper and the binder. When a rapid response team activates, binders rarely get pulled off the shelf. That said, there is real value in the thinking process and shared challenge used to create a rapid response team plan.

I recommend the experience of creating a plan be shared by the senior communications leader, the communications manager, and the team coordinator, with subject-matter experts providing guidance on specific topics. Following the draft, which can be done using an 11x17-inch piece of paper for the entire plan, it's good practice to have the plan reviewed by the chief decision-maker, deputy chief decision-maker, and legal counsel. An RRT plan can be expansive or brief, but every plan should contain five elements:

1. PRINCIPLES

The plans I design for clients contain no more than three core principles defining the way the RRT agrees to work together. For example, speed may be an important principle for a rapid response team. This principle helps remind teams to assemble quickly and to concentrate on what is important now, delaying decisions that can wait and avoiding all kinds of time-wasting hanky-twisting. Simplicity is another good one. When under pressure, tunnel vision occurs because mental bandwidth is gobbled up by dissonance, so helping team members know it's okay to communicate laconically—to say the most with the fewest words—is a best practice. Collaboration and proportionality are also good principles I've coached into RRT plans.

Transparency may not be all that helpful for protecting a brand, but some teams find it useful as a surrogate word for honesty and integrity. For proportionality, picture in your mind the geometric diagram of the Golden Mean, which resembles the spiral-shelled Nautilus. In the Message chapter, read the case story about lloyd's taco truck to see how a brand can wreck itself in short order by not communicating with proportionality. Finally, as Levick and Smith properly point out, "Crisis management is labor intensive. To manage well, you need a team..."[78] This means teamwork can also be a core principle. "Lone Ranger" conduct, such as back-channeling to outside stakeholders without the knowledge and approval of team leadership, can lead to a breach of trust within an RRT. Distrust is not a condition to deal with amid dissonance.

2. ACTIVATION

An RRT plan should specify the sequence for activating the RRT. Don't try to over-engineer activation by imagining the reasons why an RRT should activate; leave that to the judgment of the CDM and DCDM. Instead, document the method and sequence for mustering RRT members and provide them with a rapid response team card to be carried on their person at all times. In the spirit of simplicity, the card should only contain designated meeting locations (in-person and online) and specific information about how to access the location, including links and passwords, in the event an in-person meeting isn't possible. In my experience, rapid activation is the most difficult proficiency for rapid response teams to master, because they don't practice enough.

3. INCIDENT INVENTORY

Imagine what crisis events could strike your brand, then categorize the possibilities into at least three buckets: reputation incidents, safety and security incidents, and emergency incidents. Examples of each are described below.

REPUTATION INCIDENTS	SAFETY AND SECURITY INCIDENTS	EMERGENCY INCIDENTS
False claims or damaging rumors	Accidents involving injury or limited fatalities	Criminal acts, deliberate acts of terrorism, including cyberattacks
Malfeasance, misappropriation, or misconduct and related investigations	Weather-related incidents	Significant loss-of-life events, such as crashes, explosions, poisonings, or chemical breaches requiring evacuation
Kiss-cam exposures (See Chapter 11)	Regulatory violations or citations	Significant or sudden existential events, such as major financial losses
Activist protests, public disputes, or lawsuits	Product recalls or withdrawals	Outbreak/epidemiological exposure

4. PRESET MESSAGING

It's a good practice for the senior communication leader and communication team members to work through what I call, "The Dave Matthews Band Question." Remember the band's song, "What Would You Say?" Put that song and question in your head, and work through each of the issues listed in your incident inventory to predefine a few statements about each.

Preset messaging is almost never used word-for-word by a

rapid response team. Its utility is in thinking about what might be said and creating a library of words that can be drawn upon when needed. Crafting even a single sentence or sound bite in response to the Dave Matthews Band question strengthens a communication team's confidence before they're in the pressure cooker of an incident.

5. CHANNEL INVENTORY AND PASSWORDS

In the introduction, I talked about my time as the senior communication leader for the Austin Marathon, an annual 26.2-mile road race we created when I served as Motorola Semiconductor's public affairs director. I have consulted with a number of race events over the years, so I can say with confidence that they are crises-waiting-to-happen events. This makes them excellent training opportunities for anyone who wants to learn the crisis communication craft because, unfortunately, a lot of things always go wrong.

One year, a blistering winter storm blew through Austin the night before the race and coated every road and surface with ice. Of course, the City of Austin is not well-equipped for weather events like this, so the race was delayed by several hours; but not before about seven thousand runners made the hazardous trip to the starting line located on Motorola's large corporate campus in the northwest end of the city.

It was below freezing, and gusting winds punished race-ready runners who were wearing nothing but singlets and shorts. Less than two hundred feet from the starting line, our very large company cafeteria would have sheltered everyone, but there was one hitch: No one, not even site security, had the keys to the roll-up doors. It felt like the dumbest thing in the world. Over the years, that moment has been an excellent reminder to make sure every rapid response plan we create has an inventory of who has the keys to the doors an RRT will need get through, including the passwords to the digital channels the brand may need to use. These channels may include websites or web pages, social channels, email, and even on-site digital signage.

Remember in 2018, when the governor of Hawaii forgot his Twitter password following the posting of an erroneous warning that a ballistic missile was headed toward the islands? The lack of an account password meant that it took thirty-eight minutes to send out a correction. Don't be that guy.[79]

Rapid response team plans can contain much more—media contact sheets, call lists, a war room supply checklist, and even after-action questionnaires for team members—but the essentials listed above will equip your team to navigate a bad-news break, so be sure to have a rapid response team plan in your toolbox. One note: "Equipped" doesn't equate to "prepared." My staff and I regularly help prepare clients by staging and running rapid response simulations and tabletop exercises. If your RRT doesn't conduct at least annual training, consider making the case to do so. There's no better best practice than practice itself.

CHAPTER 5

THE BAD-NEWS BREAK AND THE TICK-TOCK BOX

"Bad news isn't wine. It doesn't improve with age."

—COLIN POWELL

The Rapid Response Model has a starburst interrupting the sine wave. When we diagrammed it in a workshop, fellow agency owner Ian Johnston pointed out to me that the starburst appears "just when you think everything is going fine." That's how bad news works, isn't it? The starburst represents a bad-news break and the point at which a series of decisions must be made. What do these bad-news breaks look like? Negative headlines are a good starting place.

"Dallas Cowboys Face Criticism After Partnership with Black Rifle Coffee"

—THE NEW YORK TIMES, JULY 7, 2022

"Public Utility Commission releases investigative report on CenterPoint Energy's Hurricane Beryl response"

—THE TEXAS TRIBUNE, NOVEMBER 22, 2024

"Tesla Has a Problem: Elon Musk"

—THE WALL STREET JOURNAL PODCAST, MARCH 11, 2025

"'Death Wish' Coffee Recalled Because It Can Literally Kill You"

—USA TODAY, SEPTEMBER 22, 2017

"UCLA, Northwestern, Rutgers leaders face scrutiny from lawmakers"

—THE WASHINGTON POST, MAY 23, 2024

"CrowdStrike outage is a wake-up call"

—AXIOS, JULY 23, 2024

"Why Boeing's Guilty Plea Won't Fix 737 MAX Crisis Of Trust"

—FORBES, JULY 9, 2024

"USDA report finds Boar's Head listeria outbreak was due to poor sanitation practices"

—NPR, JANUARY 11, 2025

"E. coli Outbreak Linked to Onions Served at McDonald's"

—CENTERS FOR DISEASE CONTROL AND PREVENTION, OCTOBER 22, 2024

It's a bit dated, but the Death Wish Coffee Company example is a common one. The company got nabbed for undeclared milk in its product and for containing desmethyl carbodenafil, which is chemically similar to the active ingredient in Viagra.[80] The Boar's Head incident, a listeria contamination resulting in ten deaths and sixty hospitalizations, actually drew a Class I recall card and spawned a class action lawsuit that continues to drag the brand's reputation through the muck.[81]

As challenging as these headlines may have been for the brands dealing with them, did the headlines cause significant damage? That's a question for your rapid response team to find out, but we can say each is a bad-news break, as it only takes one headline like these to create serious dissonance in the hearts and souls of consumers, employees, shareholders, and even regulators.

If you asked anyone from Boeing today if they remember the 737 MAX crisis, what are the odds they could recount several details about how the brand suffered from the experience? Pretty high, I'd bet. Dissonance events have a way of burning themselves into the memory banks of people. Interestingly, that may be less about duration in the news cycle and more about the magnitude of the dissonance.

A study called "The Lifespan of News Stories: How the News Enters and Exits the Public Consciousness" is the product of a collaboration among the data analysis company Schema, Google Trends, and the online news platform *Axios*. The team used search interest—words typed by users into a Google search bar—to gauge the level of public interest regarding a particular topic. What did they find? First, search interest is often geographically dependent. News stories about natural catastrophes attract the highest interest in the places those events affected most. The same is true for food recalls. The more geographically contained the recall, the more search interest will be locally derived.

Second, how long a news event lasts depends on how quickly it unfolds and whether the outcome was anticipated. Expected stories, such as predictable events like supermoons or the weather, move into the news cycle slowly and move out very quickly. Unexpected events, like the death of a celebrity, stay in the cycle for some time. People need to process the event, so they search for more information and keep the story alive in the news.[82]

The figures created by this study are terrific little tools that can help a brand understand its situation and move quickly to minimize news cycle time.

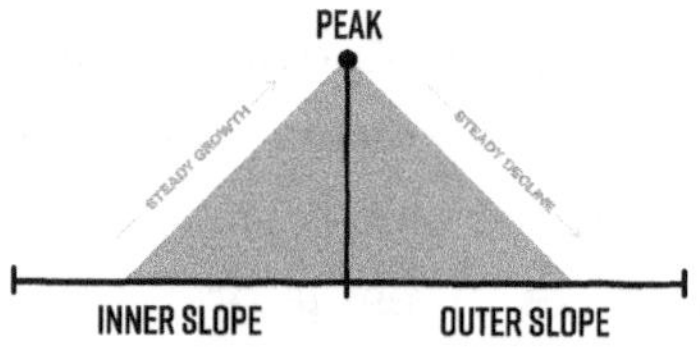

Symmetric. This reflects a news event that was anticipated ahead of time and continued to capture interest afterwards.

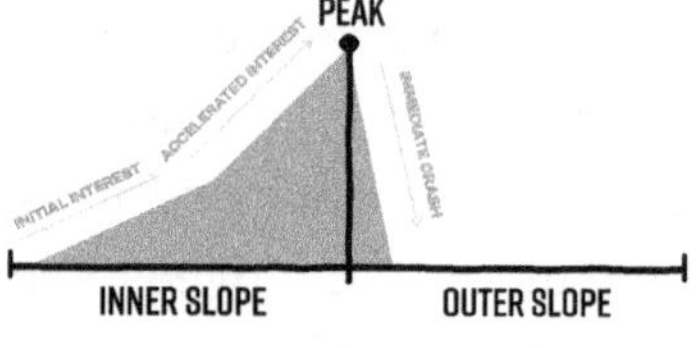

Left Skew. This is an anticipated or ongoing event that ended with a simple conclusion.

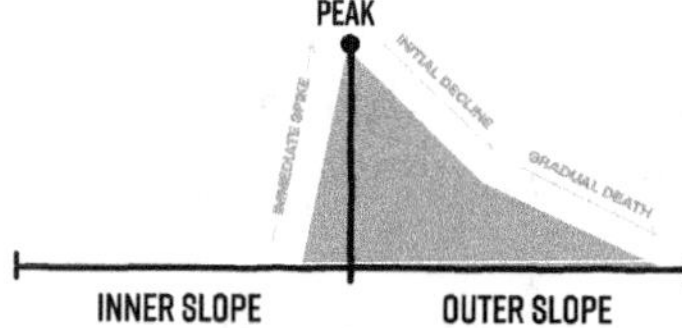

Right Skew. This reflects a sudden and unexpected news event.

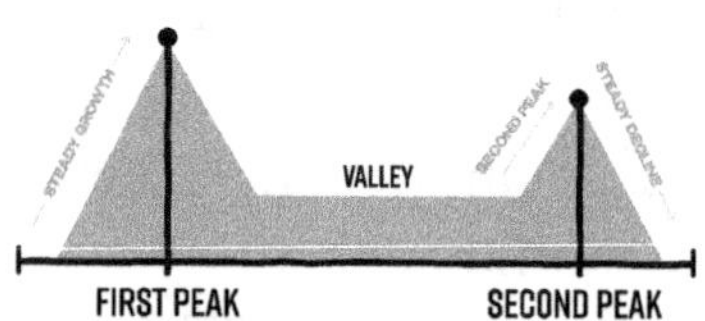

Multimodal. This is an important event that later spawned a secondary reaction or additional reporting.

An often-overlooked factor that keeps negative news in the cycle is syndication in the media business. Today, 90 percent of news reports produced in the US come from six media giants, versus about fifty media outlets in 1980.[83] Also, news syndication companies provide content to hundreds of stations, including intro scripts for newsreaders to use in their setups.[84] One story produced by one member of a media syndicate gets circulated to subscribers throughout the syndicate, garnering extensive air time, especially if it involves a product likely to be in the home pantries of the local audiences.

Imagine, then, that your brand is in a bad-news break. The headline you're reading about your brand feels shocking or unexpected, is driven by location, and is being spread through a news syndicate. Are you in a crisis? Probably. Scholars, when trying to define "crisis," have their opinions.

Jane Dutton of New York University said, "Crisis implies a perception that an individual or set of individuals faces a potentially negative outcome unless some type of corrective action is taken."[85] Keith Hearit added color to what corrective action might mean when he observed that crises question social legitimacy, requiring a public response "that seeks to distance institutional actors from their wrongdoing and reaffirm adherence to key social values."[86] A preeminent expert in this space is William Benoit, a professor of political communication at the University of Alabama at Birmingham.[87] He describes crises as "threats to image, face or reputation" which is a straightforward and practical definition.

We get more characteristics from industry players. Millar and Smith list these features of a crisis:

- Appears suddenly
- Escalates in intensity
- Demands a quick reaction
- Disrupts the organization's routine and performance
- Creates uncertainty, anxiety, and stress within and outside the organization
- Threatens the organization's reputation
- Challenges the organization's human, physical, and financial resources
- Focuses the media and other outside audiences on the organization
- Increases government and regulatory interest in the organization
- Alters the organization permanently

They summarize their thinking by saying a crisis is "a significant disruption of an organization's normal activities that stimulates extensive media coverage and public scrutiny."[88]

All these definitions come close to the mark in defining a bad-news break. It is an unwelcome, troublesome, and potentially costly event. The inclusion of "extensive media coverage and public scrutiny," which intensifies the feeling of a bad-news break, gets my vote for the most thorough definition. That said, it is missing one element Timothy Coombs pinpointed when he wrote: "A crisis is the perception of an unpredictable event that threatens important *expectancies* (emphasis mine) of stakeholders related to health, safety, environmental and economic issues, and can seriously impact an organization's performance and generate negative outcomes."[89]

As already covered, expectations set the external bar for normalcy. They create a standard against which reputation damage can be assessed.

We'll come back to a few points made by these thinkers. For now, it's smart to know that a bad-news break has a few consistent characteristics, and one of them is time. The timekeeping tool inside of the Rapid Response Model is called the Tick-Tock Box.

One of my favorite crisis communication authors, Eric Dezenhall, calls the media feeding frenzy associated with bad news the "fiasco vortex."[90] That's a great descriptive term. It reflects how rapidly bad news can be amplified and the resulting pressure on a brand to respond. The feeling of getting sucked into a vortex where you're gasping for oxygen and looking for any way out is just about right, isn't it? I wish Foghat had written a song about that feeling.

Dezenhall crystallizes it by saying, "The velocity of news has led to the tyranny of speed over accuracy. Where journalistic mistakes were once professional crimes, today they are misdemeanors, if that."[91] With this new reality, the speed with which reputation-damaging news breaks across channels can be breathtaking and ruinous. If a brand is too slow, it doesn't stand much chance of surviving.

It's not a completely new phenomenon. Jonathan Swift, a 1700s-era satirist, said, "A lie can travel halfway around the world while the truth is still putting on its shoes."[92] If you take this as a truism, then brands need to respond to bad news fast. Still, "fast" isn't perfectly clear and doesn't help us enough. We need something more objective, like a clock.

For many years, Intel Corporation used what it referred to as a "Tick-Tock Model," a clock-like label to frame its innovation cycles. Tick-Tock is a catchy phrase, and it just so happens following major news events, Tick-Tock briefings providing a chronology of events are a thing.[93] In searching dozens of publications and articles, I have found no specific answer to the question of chronology and time constraints once a crisis event occurs and a rapid response team is activated. One thing is certain: From the moment a bad-news break occurs, as a reputation manager, you are in a "Tick-Tock Box"—a frame of time where the clock is running, and your brand's reputation depends on you executing a series of actions to protect it.

Many experts advise moving quickly, rapidly, or immediately during a crisis, without offering more specific guidance. Today, your brand is judged as much on the speed of your response as the content of your communications.

Sometimes we hear pundits say that brands need to "get ahead of the story," as if that's possible when events are unexpected and everyone with a smartphone is a self-styled reporter. Just to put a fine point on how ridiculous this notion is, a Forbes Agency Council blog post entitled "13 Golden Rules of PR Crisis Management" provided thirteen crisis communication recommendations from experts. Four of the rules indicated what should be done "first":

1. "First off, don't try to cover up the PR crisis, it will only worsen the damage."
2. "First apologize, then take action."
3. "Seek first to understand the situation."
4. "Listen to your team first."[94]

None are wrong, but none are useful, because there's no time rationale provided. Why should you do any of these things first?

Why not bring a therapy pet into the room first? That's as legitimate as any of the suggestions listed above.

One reason you seldom find guidelines for specific timing of a crisis response is that timing depends on the bad news itself. Jim Haggerty says it depends on whether you've got an "exploding" or "unfolding" event.[95] Lehane, Fabiani, and Guttentag talk about the need to control the release of information at what they call "the pivot point," but offer scant guidance about the specific timing of when that point might be.[96]

Turns out, we have to draw on experience. Instinctively, we know acting with speed is good, which is why I recommend it as a first principle when developing the rapid response team plan. While speed may increase the risk of releasing inaccurate information, the benefits of a rapid initial response far outweigh any downside, especially in an exploding event.

Dr. Robert Buckman helped us begin this journey, so let's turn again to the medical profession for a model. An emergency room physician named Dr. R. Adams Cowley, founder of Baltimore's famous Shock Trauma Center at the University of Maryland Medical Center, coined the term "golden hour" to make the case that the first hour after an incident largely determines a critically injured person's odds of survival.[97]

Applying Cowley's theory to a crisis situation makes sense for several reasons.

First, in today's fiasco-vortex media environment, journalists judge any brand's response in a short amount of time. The longer it takes, the more incompetent an organization's response. Boeing learned this lesson the hard way after two of its 737 MAX jets crashed, killing 346 people.[98] Boeing was excruciatingly slow to own the narrative around these crashes. The company made useful public statements only after governments around the world had grounded the aircraft.[99]

A unique case throws a positive spotlight on the effect speed can have.

In September 2024, McDonald's faced a reputational crisis after several cases of E. coli were linked to the slivered onions on its Quarter Pounder hamburgers. In total, nearly one hundred illnesses and one death were reported, requiring thirty-four hospitalizations across fourteen states.[100]

In response, McDonald's posted timely updates on its website to keep customers informed and invested nearly $100 million in recovery efforts, emphasizing customer safety as its highest priority. When asked about the potential long-term damage to the brand, President Joe Erlinger referenced one of McDonald's founding philosophies: "If you take care of our customers, the business will take care of itself." That philosophy held true. By addressing the safety issue quickly, McDonald's moved past the incident with little prolonged negative hangover.[101]

The speed at which McDonald's responded to the crisis is especially important in today's modern age, where crises have the potential to go viral before all the facts are known.

Social media is the news source for two-thirds of American adults. One viral post, and a majority of the country has your bad news in its feed, and it doesn't matter if it's wrong.[102] Why do credible news outlets report wrong information as soon as possible? I like Molly Wood's explanation and share in her frustration. She said:

> If CNN reports [a story] twenty minutes after it showed up on Twitter (now X), the network will be skewered as pathetically behind the times. But should CNN or FOX report erroneous information in the rush to keep up, the networks will be skewered with identical glee and ruthlessness, while Reddit's slanderous and speculative threads will be congratulated as collaborative crowdsourcing that, while it may lead to devastating mistakes early on, eventually lands on the truth.[103]

A study of the social platform X entitled "The Spread of True and False News Online" found:

It took the truth about six times as long as falsehood to reach 1,500 people and 20 times as long as falsehood to reach a cascade depth of 10 [on a 20-point scale]. The truth never diffused beyond a depth of 10, falsehood, on the other hand, reached a depth of 19. Falsehood also diffused significantly more broadly and was reshared by more unique users than the truth...[104]

In crisis communication circles, the term "stealing thunder" describes how organizations can use rapid response to their benefit by being the first to actually break their own bad news. The persuasive point is that a quick response creates the impression of credibility.[105] It's also worth checking out a short study from a B2B ratings firm called Clutch. Clutch surveyed five hundred consumers about brand credibility and found brands that wait to respond to negative events are more likely to lose credibility and customers.[106] Likewise, Gene Grabowski, a partner at kGlobal who has managed large crisis events, has said, "You can't wait for the government to be the first voice heard."[107]

Finally, a rapid response demonstrates control. It isn't necessary to have all possible information when bad news breaks. It's not a sin to respond to stakeholders by saying, "We don't have answers to every question" in the early going. Instead, it's enough to simply appear willing and able to step into the bad news, leveraging what Western Michigan professor Keith Hearit refers to as the "myth of managerial rationality"—the assumption people make that professional managers can actually contain and correct a situation. Simply put, you get the benefit of the doubt, just not for long.[108]

The trouble is that abstract descriptors like "as soon as possible" aren't good enough for today's reputation managers or their rapid response teams. Effective reputation management requires activation and decision-making to exercise control over media and social media narratives that materialize within a matter of minutes.

Given the risk of conveying wildly inaccurate information, a golden hour may seem impossible and unreasonable. The critical decisions made after a bad-news break require a reasonable amount of time, because each decision is a gateway to the next. Also, each decision can be rapidly negotiated by using smart decision-making tools in the right sequence. Still, time is needed, so I have taken experiential latitude with Cowley's guidance.

During my fifteen years at Motorola, I was privileged to serve on an excellent rapid response team. Once notified of a bad-news break, we convened the team within fifteen minutes. Following a short briefing, action items were assigned, and initial communications were created, approved, and released in under two hours. The team was top-notch because, unfortunately, we had many opportunities to activate.

Your use of the Tick-Tock Box inside of the Rapid Response Model will vary depending on your organization's decision-making culture. For the sake of argument, let's use the Motorola benchmark of 120 minutes to fight through the dissonance of a bad-news break, move through the model's sequence, and begin the swing back to normalcy.

CHAPTER 6

RAPID RESPONSE TEAM ACTIVATION

"Pressure is something you feel when you don't know what the hell you're doing."

—Peyton Manning

It is impossible to know when a rapid response team might first learn about an incident. You'll recall the rapid response plans I design for clients include three incident types: reputation, safety and security, and emergency. In an emergency, on-site security is likely to initiate communication with the rapid response team as they also coordinate with first responders.

The same is true in safety and security incidents. However, reputation incidents are wild cards that may first come to light through social media monitoring or news reports. This is why rapid response teams should be populated by practitioners who know how to monitor news and social media and understand what the normal cadence of news and social media looks like for a brand.

No matter the type of incident, the clock starts ticking when a rapid response team member finds out about it and notifies the chief decision-maker.

Within zero to fifteen minutes, the chief decision-maker and deputy chief decision-maker should confer to determine whether to activate the full rapid response team. That decision can be made only through an imperfect evaluation of the situation. Generally, activation is warranted if an event is public and has the potential to cause reputational harm. If the incident is a safety or security threat or an emergency, activation is a given.

On activation, the CDM, or deputy, immediately notifies the team coordinator. The coordinator is then responsible for alerting and assembling the remaining members of the rapid response team. As noted in the chapter focused on rapid response team design and planning, multiple alert systems, such as AlertMedia's solution, make notification faster and more comprehensive than ever before.

At the fifteen-minute mark, the rapid response team should be assembled on, or in, the designated meeting area. The team coordinator calls roll, then contacts backup members for any regular RRT members not present.

These are the mechanics of zero-to-fifteen minutes. As the team assembles, be aware that a powerful emotional force has swung into action. Dissonance is now in motion and whether they realize it or not, it's creeping into the psyches of the team. This means, depending on the magnitude of the situation, team judgment may be compromised by an increasing drive to harmonize with external stakeholder expectations. Worse yet, as dissonance deepens, the restoration drive increases. This tension causes stress because not enough information is known, and not enough time is available to form an accurate picture of the events.[109]

Likewise, a growing alarm and desire to take action causes what psychologists refer to as a "scarcity trap." The NPR podcast *Hidden Brain*, hosted by Shankar Vedantam, devoted an entire episode to this phenomenon. Vedantam prefaced the episode by saying, "When you're really desperate for something, you can focus on it so obsessively there's no room for anything else. Scarcity takes a huge toll. It robs people of insight. And it helps to explain why, when we're in a hole, we sometimes dig ourselves even deeper."[110]

For the unbaptized or unprepared, dissonance-caused scarcity can lead to rash statement-making; grandstanding; or animated, time-wasting arguments among the RRT once the situation briefing begins.

In the first fifteen minutes, we're waiting for the RRT to fully assemble. It will seem like one hundred hours, and first arrivals will be anxious to ask questions. It's worth cautioning that an initial briefing of the RRT should commence only when every available team member has assembled. Starting, stopping, restarting, or repeating an initial situation briefing aggravates dissonance. Why? Because the incident story will be told in at least a slightly different way each time. The inconsistency leads to greater confusion.

Psychologist Sian Beilock discovered why our mental performance crumbles under pressure. She explained, "In stressful situations, the ability of working memory to direct attention to what's relevant is compromised. A computer is a good analogy. If you're running lots of programs at once, everything slows down. If you add worry to the mix, the attention needed to focus on the task can go awry."[111]

The deputy chief decision-maker plays an important role of convener and facilitator. While the team coordinator is busy assembling RRT members, the DCDM can put team members in a standby pattern by instructing each person as they arrive at the meeting or join a call with an instruction sounding something like this:

RRT member: "This is subject matter expert calling in. What's happening?"

DCDM: "Thanks SME. We have an incident that has warranted

activation of the rapid response team. The team coordinator is assembling as many members as possible. Once that's done, the CDM will brief us all on the situation at the same time. What you can do right now is pull out your RRT plan, including your call lists, and light up your social media accounts to track chatter. Also, we'll share a statement for your review and feedback within a few minutes. Having a second screen, separate from your phone, to view it on will make it easier for you to respond. Stand by while we get the latest information and pull everyone together."

How can you avoid dissonance-created chaos overtaking your war room? In the moment, recognize what is happening and remind the chief decision-maker of the responsibility to serve as a circuit breaker for unproductive debate. More importantly, remind the RRT they have a series of tasks to complete, in order, while a situation unfolds. These reminders are best communicated during a situation briefing.

SITUATION BRIEFING

Once the rapid response team has assembled, the chief or deputy decision-maker leads the team through an explanation of known information and a series of questions to set the response activity into motion through an easy-to-use facilitation tool called a Situation Briefing. The facilitation script might sound something like this:

Rapid response team, we have been activated due to an incident. I am going to provide a brief overview of what is known now. Once I complete the overview, I am going to ask subject matter experts on the team to provide additional information. We'll then move to complete a series of tasks: crafting and releasing a holding statement, crafting a message, preparing our messenger, then determining the method by which we'll deliver the statement to our stakeholders.

The questions asked by the CDM or DCDM may include these:

1. Has there been any threat to life or actual loss of life? Has anyone suffered any injuries or negative health effects?
2. Has an evacuation been ordered? Has any unplanned release into or damage to the environment occurred?
3. Has any significant disruption to operations, buildings, IT, data, utilities, or facilities occurred?
4. Have first responders been activated?
5. Are government officials/regulators involved, or do we need to inform them?
6. Is media on the scene or in contact?
7. What is happening on social media?
8. What are the most important things we don't know at this moment?
9. What appears to be the root cause? Is it internal—our people or our responsibility—or is the cause external?
10. Does the root cause appear to be intentional or unintentional?

Questions #9 and #10 above set up an important decision explained in the Message chapter.

CHAPTER 7

HOLDING STATEMENT

"What is there so fearful as the expectation of evil tidings delayed? Misery is a more welcome visitant when she comes in her darkest guise and wraps us in perpetual black, for then the heart no longer sickens with disappointed hope."

—MARY SHELLEY

The first order of business is to brief the rapid response team on the incident and get the team into alignment. The second order of business is to answer the Dave Matthews Band question (What would you say?) by crafting a holding statement to stakeholders.

Before jumping headlong into writing up statements, though, it's useful to bring perspective to the moment. For that, we turn to another useful tool.

W. Timothy Coombs presented his Crisis Type Matrix in a 1995 paper entitled, "Choosing the Right Words: The Development of Guidelines for the Selection of the 'Appropriate' Crisis-Response Strategies."[112] When I'm in a war room with a rapid response team and the Tick-Tock Box tells us it's time to discuss a holding statement, this is the tool I pull from my toolbox to coach the team toward an initial opinion about the appropriate shape of a holding statement.

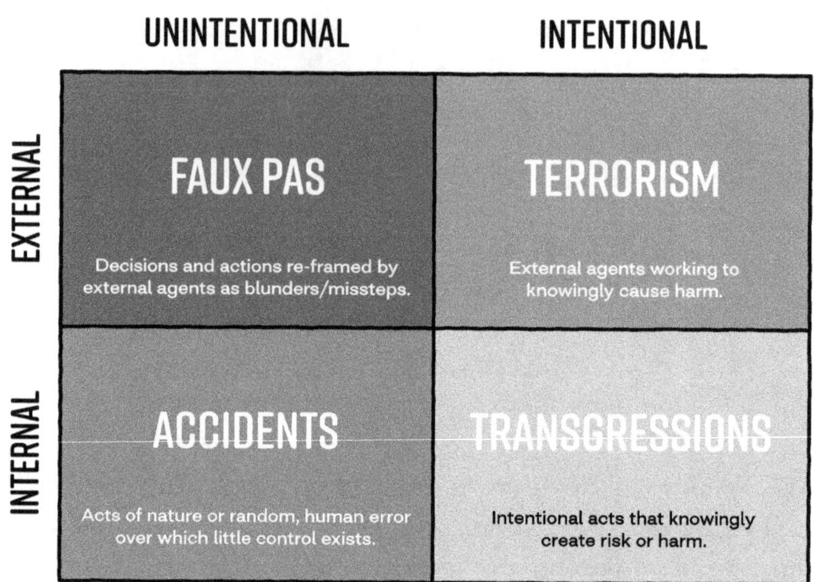

The first question, asked initially during the rapid response team briefing, is, "Was the incident caused by someone or something inside or outside of the brand's control?" If external, the messaging has to explain the role the outside actor(s) played in creating the crisis. If internal, you are likely facing culpability caused by your brand's own actions.

Second question, "Was the crisis incident unintentional or intentional?" If it was unintentional, then the organization did not purposely initiate the unfolding events. No malicious intent or motive exists. The absence of a motive shapes a message in a dramatically different way than when a motive exists. If the crisis incident was intentional, that implies control, and a player who knowingly put events into motion.

With only two questions, you can label a crisis event. Why is that important? It's because labels are powerful shapers of the psyche, setting a tone for more extensive messaging. American sociologist Howard Becker, in his book *Outsiders: Studies in the Sociology of Deviance*,[113] contends that human behavior is significantly influenced by the way other members of society label the behaviors. The same is true of a crisis incident. Once people label it, the shape of a message begins to appear. In his 2x2, Coombs provides us with four labels:

FAUX PAS

This is an unintentional act: "an external agent tries to transform into a crisis."[114] For example, a brand may change its product. Take Coca-Cola, which was mired in a reputational crisis for seventy-nine days in 1985 following the rollout of New Coke. Coca-Cola thought it was doing what consumers wanted. Nearly 200,000 taste tests had supported it; therefore, it was not Coca-Cola's intention to do wrong. But the public, the external agents in this case, erupted and formed protest groups. One was called the "Society for the Preservation of the Real Thing." Another dubbed itself the "Old Cola Drinkers of America." The company was getting fifteen hundred calls a day on its consumer hotline (mostly angry, by press accounts), compared with four hundred a day before the rollout.[115] In Coombs's model, Coca-Cola had committed a *faux pas*—a blunder, a goof up, a mistake. The tone inside this cell can include expressions of embarrassment, frustration, astonishment, empathy, or aggravation, each of which can be useful in bringing shape to a message.

ACCIDENTS

An accident is unintentional but caused internally by someone in your organization. Product defects and employee injuries fit this category. Accidents are typically caused by strange, often unforeseeable circumstances. In April 2019, for example, a line worker named Jill Greninger was operating a commercial meat-grinding machine at the Economy Locker Storage Company, when she fell into it. The Lycoming County Coroner said, "This is just a tragedy. She died inside the moving machine."[116] Take a moment to imagine how you would feel if you had to craft and deliver a statement about Greninger's death. You would likely want to sound sympathetic and upset as well as determined it never happens again. The "tragedy" label helps shape the incident and subsequent messaging.

TRANSGRESSIONS

A transgression, while internal, bears the fingerprints of intentionality. As Hearit puts it, "Contrary to popular belief, most crises are not the result of an external psychopath but instead are self-generated, the result of internal screw ups on the part of the companies... Organizations are more often than not the victims of their own misdeeds."[117]

A different meat-grinder incident clearly illustrates the difference between an accident and a transgression. In June 2003, thirty-four-year-old Daniel Romero Cruz died while cleaning a Butcher Boy Meat Grinder-Mixer at Michael Angelo's Gourmet Foods in Round Rock, Texas. This would be a tragic accident except that a few years before, in different inspections, the US Occupational Health and Safety Administration (OSHA) cited Michael Angelo's for fifty-six alleged safety violations and an ammonia release. The federal agency socked the company with penalties totaling $382,500 because investigators found it had deliberately bypassed safety mechanisms on some machines to speed up production and machinery maintenance. The company was cited for two "willful" safety violations, meaning it had intentionally disregarded safety protocols and "knew or should have known of the hazard."[118]

Michael Angelo's couldn't deny their record of past performance. It knowingly placed workers and the public at risk and, therefore, committed a transgression. In this cell of the 2x2, you can select a tone ranging from shock and surprise to betrayal and indignation, the latter two of which we'll explore in the next chapter.

One of the biggest fraud cases in recent history stems from transgression. Sam Bankman-Fried, founder of the cryptocurrency exchange FTX and the cryptocurrency trading firm Alameda Research, was found guilty of misappropriating billions of dollars of customer funds deposited with FTX, defrauding the investors of FTX of more than $1.7 billion, and defrauding lenders to Alameda of more than $1.3 billion. He was sentenced to twenty-five years in prison and three years of supervised release and ordered to pay $11 billion in forfeiture for his orchestration of multiple fraudulent schemes.[119]

TERRORISM

Brands may feel immune to this label because of the startling nature of the term. The label is appropriate, though, as it refers to "intentional action taken by external actors…designed to harm the organization."[120] The 2021 Colonial Pipeline ransomware attack initiated by the cybercriminal group DarkSide is a good example of an external and intentional crisis. The cyberattack caused fuel shortages across the northeastern US, resulting in panic buying and gas price spikes.[121] To mitigate the situation, President Biden declared a state of emergency until pipeline service was restored.[122]

Here's a dated example, but I use it because the response was just weird, even though the crisis fit perfectly within the terrorism label box. In 1986, the US Food and Drug Administration received about 140 reports of glass in Gerber baby food. The subsequent investigation confirmed twenty-one cases of tampering. At the time, Gerber spokesperson L. James Lovejoy said the company, with the FDA's support, believed there was "absolutely no indication that there is a problem" with its products and had no plans to withdraw them. Then, when the State of Maryland banned Gerber strained peaches in response to the scare, Gerber sued the state. In an updated article, *The Washington Post* reported: "Gerber also has said it is not responsible for breakage that may occur when glass containers are mishandled in transit. 'It's out of our hands once the jars have left the factory,' said Gerber spokeswoman Grace Durr."[123]

Ultimately, the FDA concluded pieces of glass were intentionally put into the baby food after it reached retail outlets. Why, though, was the company unwilling to use the terrorism label to shape the thinking about its messaging instead of just saying it wasn't their problem? Today, Gerber's response would spark outrage, as consumers expect a company to own every aspect of their product's life cycle. But even more than forty years ago, wouldn't it have been easier to swing the narrative around to claim the victim position rather than denying a problem existed?

Coombs's Crisis Type Matrix is useful at the very outset of a crisis incident when you have only initial sketchy information. By thinking through the matrix and applying a label to an incident, you can craft an appropriate and proportional holding statement very quickly and for that, it is an essential tool for your response toolbox.

HOLDING STATEMENT TEMPLATE

In woodworking, a jig is a device, a template that guides a tool or a workpiece, ensuring accuracy, repeatability, and safety for repetitive tasks, such as cutting, drilling, and joining. We'll take that metaphor and turn it into another useful tool.

Typically, holding statements are one paragraph long, crafted for the sole purpose of informing stakeholders you are aware an event has occurred and are actively working to assess it. One of the great attributes of holding statements is that they can be crafted in anticipation of a bad-news break. This is a task for a small group, typically the communications team members, who don't mind having several hours over several days ruined by trying to imagine worst-case scenarios for your brand.

Holding statements may confirm known facts and even contain expressions of empathy if the situation warrants. Two situations that obviously call for empathetic messaging are loss of life and physical injury to people. Showing you understand the severity of what has happened demonstrates compassion, concern, and humanity.

Holding statements can buy you only so much time, so it's smart to include an indication of when you expect to provide more comprehensive information. They can also steer reporters to a contact name, number, and/or email address for more information. Properly crafted holding statements never contain speculation and never respond to rumors or unconfirmed reports.

A few examples may help:

1. "An emergency has occurred at our location. First responders have been alerted to ensure the safety of staff and the facility. We appreciate their efforts and will continue to closely coordinate our response with them. At present, our team is working to determine the extent of the incident. For now, reporters should confine themselves and any vehicles to the rear of the parking area. Our communication manager plans to visit that area every hour to provide updates."

2. "An incident involving several people working at our refinery has occurred. We are working as quickly as possible to understand the circumstances of this event. When a more complete picture of the situation emerges, we will share additional information. For now, reporters should make way for first responders and maintain a safe distance from the facility. We intend to provide updates regularly."

3. "A recall of (a specified product) is underway. We are working closely with regulatory officials and notifying all affected retailers. Consumers who bought this product should immediately dispose of it or call our hotline if they are unsure whether it is included in the recall. This is a rare event for our brand, as we pride ourselves on making high-quality products. At present, our priority is to locate all products involved to assure consumer safety. We will communicate more information as it becomes available."

These examples share a few important characteristics:

- Each is straightforward with little embellishment.
- Each is fewer than one hundred words. This isn't a hard-and-fast rule, but it's a good guideline to avoid providing too much information.
- Each is formulated in the present tense. Holding statements should never indicate future decision-making—only that more information is forthcoming.
- Each minimizes the use of negative words. Did someone die in the event? While sanitized words like "incident" may feel like you are trivializing death, caution is warranted. Only a coroner can officially declare a person dead. Give your brand a little extra time by embracing the fact that, in this moment, you do not have every piece of information.
- Each uses ambiguous, context-setting language to provide perspective and keep options open. A good holding statement communicates nothing that may be proven inaccurate or need correction in subsequent updates—no numbers, few specifics, and no names, including the brand's name. Use the first-person point of view (words like "we" and "us") instead of proper nouns.
- None rushes to apologize.

Reassuring stakeholders you are aware of an issue and addressing it buys your rapid response team time to prepare more comprehensive messaging, and time is your most challenging constraint. For your rapid response team, releasing a holding statement taps the brakes on the dissonance plunge, because it restores some feeling of control and decisiveness amid a foggy situation.

CHAPTER 8

MESSAGE

"Make your mess your message. Make your test your testimony."
—Pastor Joel Osteen

Following Charlie Munger's guidance, the Rapid Response Model has a unique feature: It lattices models, frameworks, and tools together. Picture a kinetic mobile—a work of art hanging from a ceiling with smaller elements suspended from the larger ones, all hanging from a fixed point at the top. This latticing becomes more evident in the Message stage, where the Coombs model is built upon by another indispensable tool––the Image Repair Typology developed by William Benoit, reimagined by me as an easier-to-follow flowchart.

Several authors have opined about messaging in a crisis: Robert Buckman, in his book *How to Break Bad News: A Guide for Health Care Professionals*; Steven Fink, in his book *Crisis Communication: The Definitive Guide to Managing the Message*; and former CNN reporter Jeff Ansell, in his book *When the Headline Is You: An Insider's Guide to Handling the Media*, to name a few. What they share is that the Message stage of the Rapid Response Model diagram is particularly important, because the words crafted in this phase set a narrative capable of protecting a brand from further reputational damage.

The right words can make the difference between short-term bad news and long-term reputational damage. A key hypothesis of crisis communication is that message quality is essential, and the better job we do of responding to bad-news breaks, the faster we can move our brand out of a negative, white-hot spotlight.

How should a good message be structured? Fink argued that bad news should be delivered calmly, honestly, succinctly, and factually.[124] He advocates using the "sandwich technique," a method of saying something positive, then something negative, and then something reassuring. Mary Kay Ash, founder of Mary Kay Cosmetics, gets original credit for this technique. She called it her "feedback sandwich."[125] However, I have never seen this technique work effectively in a crisis situation. Time doesn't allow for it; it is akin to putting lipstick on a pig, as the saying goes, and research supports taking a different tack.

Here's a question you've probably been asked a few hundred times: "I've got good news and bad news. Which do you want to hear first?"

In his book *When: The Scientific Secrets of Perfect Timing*, Daniel Pink says he used to break good news to employees before bad news. "My instinct has been to spread a downy duvet of good feeling to cushion the coming hammer blow," he says. "My instinct, alas, has been dead wrong."[126] Pink elaborated in an interview with *The Washington Post*: "The research tells us this very, very clearly. If you ask people what they prefer, four out of five prefer getting the bad news first. The reason has to do with endings. Given the choice, human beings prefer endings that elevate. We prefer endings that go up, that have a rising sequence rather than a declining sequence."[127] I think this is terrific advice and recommend Pink's book to you. It's a great read as it'll help you appreciate the critical nature of sequence.

How, along with Ash and Fink, can this provide us guidance on creating messages in a crisis? Jeff Ansell gives a little advice. In his book, he advises us to "be accessible and forthcoming."[128]

Unfortunately, his advice, along with those noted above, doesn't provide enough guidance. We need to know what ideas to put into words, proportional to the incident. But how do we know if we're saying the right things at the right times in the right ways? What options are available, and how do we know we've chosen correctly, especially when the lawyers in the war room are advising "no comment" and bloviating about how "we don't try cases in the press!"

Objections like that reaffirm the presence of dissonance. The fact is, brands in crisis are routinely tried by the news media in the court of public opinion days, weeks, or months before the first courtroom motion is filed.

Brand managers know their responsibility is to get their brand to high ground faster than the legal process will allow. How to get there? You may say, "I know. Let's issue an apology!" Perfect. You'll say you're sorry, and everything will be better? While an apology can be an effective messaging technique, any competent reputation manager knows when the proverbial spaghetti hits the fan, and your brand gets splattered with goo, saying "sorry" at the wrong time is a wasted effort and often brings more trouble.

IMAGE REPAIR TYPOLOGY

After cycling through the questions in Coombs's 2x2 for the holding statement, two additional questions materialize:

1. Is my brand being blamed for something? Are we rightly or wrongly being held responsible for acts we allegedly performed, ordered, encouraged, facilitated, or permitted; alleged acts of omission; or alleged acts of poor performance?
2. Does the public, or a portion of the public, perceive the acts to be offensive?

If the answer to these questions is yes, then pull Benoit's Image Repair Typology out of the toolbox and use it to select a message starting point. Benoit has been a leading scholar in the area of crisis communication for decades, with much of his work framed around apologia, the rhetoric of defense. His book *Accounts, Excuses, and Apologies: Image Repair Theory and Research* may be the most comprehensive decision-logic tool available to reputation managers, and it's always the second one I grab from my toolbox to help a rapid response team make messaging decisions.

If events have not yet unfolded with enough detail to assess the quick questions above, the natural tendency is to wait. Benoit might agree. He says, "One cannot expect a successful image repair effort without clearly understanding the attacks one faces."[129] Understood. However, inside the Tick-Tock Box, time is not on our side. Stakeholders, including the media, are busy making up their own stories, so the task is to develop a brand-protecting narrative based on the shape of the holding statement and the best available information.

Benoit presents his Image Repair Typology in table form. The way he organizes and stacks his ideas prompts me to view the choices offered as a sequence, and sequences make great models, so I have reimagined Benoit's table into a flowchart model.

If you answered yes to the two questions above, then use this model by asking a third crucial question: Given the situation, should our brand reject or accept blame for the incident?

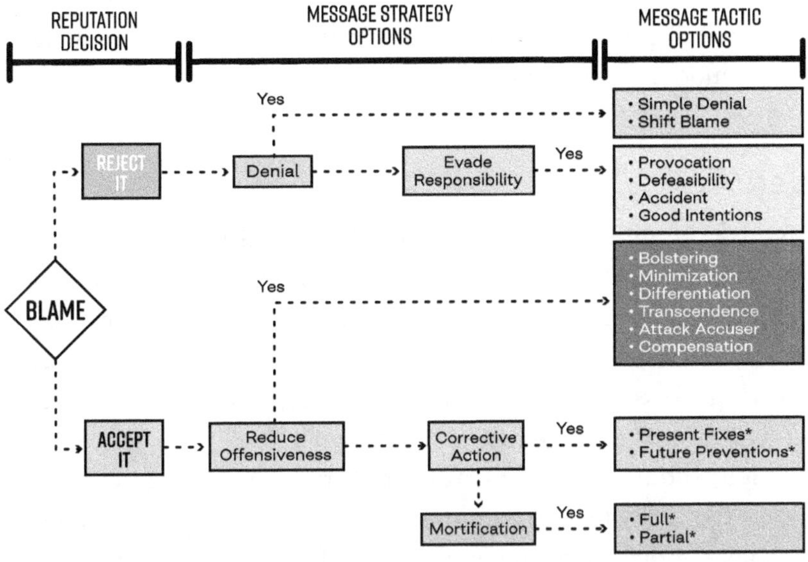

Remember the principles of a good model? Two of them come into full view when studying Benoit's typology: (1) make the complex simple and (2) models are not processes, although some of the best contain sequences that can help make sense of the world. This is a smart representation, but not for aesthetics alone. Inside the Tick-Tock Box, time is short. Having a tool that allows rapid selection of an appropriate shape is essential to shaping that message.

"Shape" is a word I've put into play several times, so I will give credit where it is due. The idea comes from the author Kurt Vonnegut, who said, "The fundamental idea is that stories have shapes which can be drawn on graph paper, and that the shape of a given society's stories is at least as interesting as the shape of its pots or spearheads."[130] I'm a Vonnegut fan because he thought about stories as models. If you feel the same, visit the website No Film School where you'll find Vonnegut's "shapes of stories" illustrated.[131]

The best way to understand Benoit's thinking about reputation defense is to buy his book and plunge into Image Repair Typology yourself. Short of that, the notes below explain more about each of the model's elements.

DENIAL

Use Denial when whatever allegation is being leveled at your brand is simply not true. You can add more information or explanation, like an alibi, if the situation allows. If outright denial isn't an option, move to the second tactic under this strategy—"blame shifting." To use blame shifting effectively, you need a marvelous and often-used device called a "scapegoat."

Scapegoats are wonderful reputation defenders. They can range from physical to personal to spiritual. We've all used them, and academics have put considerable thought into what makes a good scapegoat. Ott and Aoki observed, "Scapegoating alienates and sacrifices one member of a community in order to purify a shared problem."[132] That's good, but for my money, no one has nailed this subject better than Charlie Campbell in his book *Scapegoat: A History of Blaming Other People*.[133] Running a close second is *Mistakes Were Made (but Not by Me)*, by Carol Tavris and Elliot Aronson.[134] Both are chock-full of terrific information about scapegoats and the available types, including religious, sexual, and political; even actual goats themselves and proverbial sacrificial lambs are talked about.

My G.O.A.T. scapegoat is "circumstance." It can be made responsible for virtually everything that goes wrong everywhere, so blame the hell out of it whenever you need a fall guy. An example of this came from ERCOT, the Electric Reliability Council of Texas, when it faced criticism after a deadly power grid failure in Texas.

ERCOT is the organization responsible for managing the flow of power in Texas. In February 2021, a severe winter storm named Uri swept through Texas, triggering a statewide power loss. As many Texans turned on the heat to stay warm, electricity demand exceeded the state's generation capacity. To manage the strain on the electric grid, ERCOT initiated rolling blackouts across the state. This left over 4.8 million customers without power as temperatures plummeted, resulting in 246 deaths.[135]

What was ERCOT's messaging during this catastrophe? ERCOT and Texas state leaders attempted to reject blame using scapegoating.

During an interview with FOX News, Governor Greg Abbott claimed that the source of the failure was the state's renewable energy assets, specifically the frozen wind turbines in West Texas. In doing this, he tied the crisis to a broader political debate over "the Green New Deal" and said that the failure "shows how the Green New Deal would be a deadly deal for the United States of America." He said, "Our wind and our solar got shut down," which "thrust Texas into a situation where it was lacking power on a statewide basis."[136]

Investigations later revealed that the main cause of the crisis actually stemmed from failures to winterize the state's natural gas pipeline infrastructure, so the public's reaction to Governor Abbott's claims was less than enthusiastic. Scapegoating can be an effective tool, but like others, it has to be used intelligently.

EVADING RESPONSIBILITY

A more nuanced way to reject blame is to invoke the word "because." The provocation and defeasibility tactics in the Image Repair Typology rely on evading responsibility by positioning actions as responses to other wrongful acts. Defeasibility provides a way to claim that a lack of information or control over a situation is blameworthy. Defeasibility is most useful when unforeseen actions can be cited as a reason for taking an action, although it is not a direct denial.

Right out of Coombs's matrix, accident and good intentions anchor the other Evading Responsibility options. Neither denies that an incident has occurred; in fact, both work to reduce culpability. Regarding good intentions, Benoit explains, "People who do bad while trying to do good are usually not blamed as much as those who intend to do bad."[137]

REDUCING OFFENSIVENESS

McDonald's has been good in crises, and they have been bad. Back in 2002, McDonald's issued this statement: "Mistakes were made in communicating to the public and customers about the ingredients in our French fries and hash browns." McDonald's had failed to inform Hindus and other vegetarians that the "natural flavoring" in their potatoes came from beef tallow. After apologizing, the company donated $10 million to Hindu and other groups to settle lawsuits filed against the chain for the mislabeling.[138] Who made the mistakes? That's an interesting question, but the company obviously moved across the transom from blame-rejection strategies into blame-acceptance, landing squarely in the realm of reducing offensiveness.

Reducing Offensiveness can take several tactical forms, but choosing this path in the model comes with a caveat: Once you select an accept-blame strategy, it is very difficult to walk back to an outright reject-blame footing. That said, each tactic deserves an explanation, as each has important messaging power.

BOLSTERING

Use this technique to remind the public of all the good your brand has done in the past. It's one to combine with other tactics.

MINIMIZATION

Is the crisis really as bad as what is being portrayed in the news? If not, put this technique to use. It's especially helpful in anticipating what the news will blow out of proportion and inoculating your brand against media exaggerations.

DIFFERENTIATION

Can you create a comparison to put the incident into perspective? Maybe instead of stealing money, your client "borrowed" it? It may be a stretch, but it could be worth making that stretch to reduce the magnitude presented by a reputation challenge.

TRANSCENDENCE

Context is the key to this technique. Robin Hood stole from the rich, which was bad. But since he gave it to the poor, it was generally seen as cool. Positive context can reduce the magnitude of a crisis. I've always been a fan of the axiom, "One way to solve your problem is to get a bigger problem." Transcendence creates the opportunity for this shift to take place.

ATTACK ACCUSER

By smearing the credibility of an accuser, you can take away some of the sting of their accusations. You can also assume the position of victim to deflect blame and show the accuser's judgment is questionable. Almost every politician uses this technique, no matter the situation.

COMPENSATION

If none of the above techniques for reducing offensiveness work, you might try paying your way out. This appears to be what McDonald's did with its tallow problem, and it was an ending with a twist. In the early stages of the crisis, when the lawsuit for misleading labeling was filed, the company put out a statement:

"While we are not familiar with the details of the litigation filed in Seattle, we have never made any vegetarian claims about our French fries or any other product." That's a denial.

The lawsuit filed on behalf of vegetarians said the statement contradicted previous claims McDonald's had made assuring customers it used 100 percent vegetable oil for its fries. What to say next? McDonald's followed up with another statement saying "beef flavoring is added during potato processing at the plant and is standard in making French fries. The natural flavoring consists of a minuscule amount of beef extract. These fries are then shipped to our restaurants. Our French fries are cooked in vegetable oil at our restaurants."[139] Wait a minute, that response appears to be minimization, which is a flip-flop from one side of Image Repair to the other. The $10 million donation to Hindu groups and others? That's Compensation. Not good.

If you're not having to work this kind of crisis, it's fun to use Benoit's Image Repair Typology to perform forensics on the messaging brands use when they get in trouble. Test yourself on this one:

Several years ago, Bud Light added this copy to its label: "The perfect beer for removing 'No' from your vocabulary for the night." This was clearly an unacceptable choice of words. The brand received significant blowback, as it was accused of promoting everything from sexual assault to drunk driving.[140] What would have been the best available response at the time?

Dave Matthews Band question time: Using the options above—denial, evading responsibility, or reducing offensiveness—what would you say? If you conclude that none of the options discussed so far works for the Bud Light situation, you're ready to learn about the final two elements of Benoit's Image Repair Typology.

CORRECTIVE ACTION

This is a widely used strategy, but it has a few dimensions worth unpacking. In general, Corrective Action messaging explains how a brand will make things right in the wake of an accident or transgression. "Right" is a surrogate term for "normal," and "normal" is the target destination when dissonance floods the zone. It's also the space that represents the public's expectations of what your brand's behavior should be.

In March 2019, Tyson Foods recalled 69,000 pounds of frozen, ready-to-eat chicken strips potentially contaminated with metal fragments. Two months later, in May, the US Department of Agriculture Food Safety and Inspection Service (FSIS) expanded the recall to nearly twelve million pounds, because consumers kept finding pieces of metal in the chicken and reporting oral injuries. Tyson's frustration with the months-long recall is evident in a statement attributed to Barbara Masters, vice president of regulatory food policy, food and agriculture for Tyson Foods:

> Consumers expect that the food they eat is safe. In their best interest and in an abundance of caution we're taking quick and decisive action to expand this recall. Our company is taking corrective action at the location that makes these products. We have discontinued use of the specific equipment believed to be associated with the metal fragments, and we will be installing metal-detecting X-ray machinery to replace the plant's existing metal-detection system.[141]

Masters's statement is a well-constructed, present-tense account of the actions Tyson took in the moment to make things right. Nicely played.

The August 2018 edition of *Eater* magazine featured an article by Brenna Houck and Dana Hatic entitled "Why Does It Seem Like Everyone Is Getting Sick from Salad?"[142] The focus was on a series of recalls of salad products found to be contaminated by E. coli and an intestinal parasite called cyclospora. McDonald's, Trader Joe's, Kroger, and Walgreens had pulled all salad products from their shelves over the preceding several months. Those recalls, combined with a nationwide recall of romaine lettuce implemented the previous April, had stripped most popular salad products from grocery shelves. In fact, the romaine recall represented the largest multistate foodborne E. coli outbreak in more than a decade, when 172 people were sickened in thirty-two states, and one person in California died.[143] The McDonald's recall alone involved 395 illnesses across fifteen states.[144]

Jean Halloran, director of food policy initiatives at Consumer Reports, had this to say about the Food and Drug Administration's response: "It's good that the FDA has clearly laid out what it does and does not know about this outbreak. But the agency should also be taking steps to keep E. coli out of lettuce in the future, including issuing its long-delayed water quality rules."[145]

Halloran called for the industry to make statements about future actions designed to prevent problems from occurring. Future preventative actions can be added to present fixes to reinforce a Corrective Action message. Benoit supports this: "Those accused of wrongdoing...frequently deny responsibility, shift blame, and offer justifications or excuses. However, corrective action is clearly oriented to the future."[146]

Another way to strengthen Corrective Action messages is to craft them in triad form—not more than three at any given time.

Triads—the grammatically correct label is tricolons—convey a message with a beginning, middle, and end. Storytelling follows this structure. When used in Corrective Action messaging, a triad gives stakeholders a sense that the list of past, present, and future actions is comprehensive. As Mark Forsyth puts it, "When you finish a tricolon, you finish because there is nothing more to say. You've said it all. The list is complete. These are the final words. Two is only a pair, and four is all wrong."[147] Triads provide a symbolic shorthand for progress toward a goal—the gradual process of fixing things and finding the best way to move forward.

Four types of triads are at our disposal: cumulative, ascending, contrasting, and dialectical. Ascending triads are especially effective. They present each corrective action as a positive step, in crescendo-like fashion with each step being a little more important than the last.[148] Entire works have been dedicated to exploring triads, ranging from fairy tales—*The Three Little Pigs, Goldilocks and the Three Bears*—to sacred symbolism like the Father, the Son, and the Holy Spirit, and hymns like *We Three Kings from Orient Are*, to literature (three ghosts in Dickens's *A Christmas Carol*, three witches in Shakespeare's *Hamlet*), to rhetorical phrases ("blood, sweat, and tears"; "life, liberty, and the pursuit of happiness"). The power of thoughtfully crafted corrective action statements is magnified when well-designed triads are applied.

MORTIFICATION

I'm not a fan of superfluous apologies. They sound something like this: "Management offers its apologies for the inconvenience to our customers who may have been offended by the events that occurred." First of all, when an apology is from no one, to no one, it's hollow. Second, apologizing for things totally beyond one's control is dumb. It's no secret brands make mistakes. When expectations of service, performance, or safety don't live up to promises made, Mortification may be in order, but running head-over-heels toward apologies can lead to trouble. A food trailer business named lloyd provides a cautionary tale.

The team at lloyd decided to serve tacos to federal detention workers in Batavia, New York, just east of Buffalo. Some social media users jumped on lloyd about how bad it was to serve oppressive immigration and detention workers, vowing to never eat their tacos again. A co-founder, Pete Cimino, issued this statement in response:

Yesterday, we made an honest mistake by serving lunch at the federal detention facility in Batavia.

We're sorry.

A few weeks ago, we received a request to serve at the facility and processed it using our standard intake procedure. Typically, that process helps us make business decisions we are proud of. Unfortunately, in this case, it did the opposite.

lloyd has deep ties to the immigrant and refugee communities in Buffalo. We work closely with Jericho Road and the International Institute of Buffalo as part of our hiring and recruitment efforts, and every year we look forward to participating in the Buffalo Without Borders fundraiser.

There is no excuse for what happened and we have already begun to update our internal procedures to ensure future truck stops and events align with our company's values. As part of our efforts to make amends and learn from this experience, we are donating all of the sales from yesterday's service to Justice for Migrant Families WNY.

We know that words cannot change the past and a donation doesn't make up for our lapse in judgment. Only time and future actions can show our commitment to being a more thoughtful company. Today, we begin that journey.

We're sorry, Buffalo. You deserve better.

Wow! That was a full heap of an apology, wasn't it? What happened next? You may not be surprised that Cimino was compelled to issue yet another apology after other social media users blew up about his over-the-top genuflection to the immigrant-rights crowd. His follow-up read:

Chris [Dorsaneo, the co-owner] and I want to fully and sincerely apologize for our past statement after our truck's visit to the federal detention facility in Batavia last week. Our statement was hastily made, and we reacted too quickly to criticism we received for that visit.[149]

If you're shaking your head in disbelief about this case, it's understandable, and yet, apologies get sprayed into the news and social media every day without much thought. A deeper dive into this device, therefore, is in order. Step back for a moment and recognize that apologies can be exceptional rhetorical tools. The challenge, as Benoit cautions, is that they are "particularly complex," so much so that entire websites like PerfectApology.com are devoted to the idea.[150]

First things first: What is an apology? The experts who have weighed in on this question don't agree on one definition. Nicholas Tavuchis thinks of apologies as moral syllogisms and believes they follow a three-step sequence: (1) a call to apologize, where the offender and the offended recognize an apology is in order; (2) naming the offense and uttering apologetic words; and (3) the response, which is the acceptance, rejection, or discussion of the apology made.[151] The structure is simple, but given how complex apologies can be, we should be as comprehensive as possible. By combining a few more sources, the elements of a full apology come into view as follows:

1. Statement of remorse
2. Account or description of events
3. Acknowledgment of the harm or damage caused
4. Offer of reparation
5. Explicit statement of responsibility
6. Request for forgiveness
7. Self-castigation (admitting shame or embarrassment)
8. Promise not to repeat the offense by getting better/being better[152]

Second, should apologies be used? Eric Dezenhall thinks so. He says, "An apology works when a transaction occurs whereby something small is surrendered (pride) but something of value—such as one's freedom—is preserved."[153] Nicolaus Mills, a professor of American studies at Sarah Lawrence College, agrees. In an article for *Dissent* magazine, "The New Culture of Apology," he cites more than a dozen examples of mea culpas, ranging from Coors Brewing Company to the Catholic Church, observing: "The value of the new culture of apology is not that it makes utopia possible. It is that it offers a way of freeing ourselves from the cycle of accusation and counteraccusation that wrongdoing inevitably imposes."[154]

This makes sense especially because apologies are often viewed as admissions of guilt. Lauren Bloom researched this question and wrote, "...some experts estimate that the average family of four pays over $2,000 per year in hidden costs associated with business litigation."[155]

When the lawyer on your rapid response team raises a stink about the liability you could incur by issuing an apology and having it used as an admission of guilt, they have a point. Apologizing after an accident, especially one involving injury, poses potential risk for a brand.

Ample evidence to the contrary also exists. In fact, an effective apology can contribute to a favorable resolution in the court of public opinion, because it demonstrates the brand's alignment with public expectations of morally acceptable behavior. This is especially useful if the brand is caught red-handed doing something inappropriate that cannot be blamed on others.

After a local natural gas distribution company was involved in a house explosion incident, I was called in to support the rapid response team's deliberations. The legal members of the team strongly opposed issuing a public apology. After listening for some time to all the risks, the head of corporate communications (with elevated volume) said, "Hey! A person has been killed. It was a terrible accident. Tell me how much more the check we're going to write is going to be if we admit that we're human and that we're terribly sorry?!" It was a courageous stand, and enough research shows it was a smart question leading to a sound decision.

As Patel and Reinsch put it, "The risks of making an apology are low and the potential reward is high. If the apology is accepted... retaliation or animosity [may be] eradicated. If the apology is rejected, the apologizing party is left in the same position of expecting retaliation and is no worse off."[156] That's a fairly low threshold for justifying an apology. There is ample evidence of plaintiffs who have accepted lesser settlements when the offers have included apologies. Further, while an apology may be admitted into evidence to support an injured party's claim, admissibility is never synonymous with proof of guilt, and judges and juries tend to regard apologies favorably.[157] A famous case—it has its own Wikipedia page and HBO documentary—illustrates the argument.

Here's an interesting example. An elderly woman named Stella Liebeck spilled a cup of hot McDonald's coffee in her lap while riding in a car. She suffered severe burns that required skin grafts. Her family repeatedly attempted to settle the case, asking for $20,000 to cover $11,000 in medical expenses, plus lost income. McDonald's legal team refused, countering with an offer of $800. The family took the company to court.

The evidence at trial revealed that the restaurant did indeed regularly serve dangerously hot coffee. In fact, discovery uncovered that McDonald's had registered more than seven hundred complaints about burns caused by its hot beverages over the previous ten years. The jury awarded the victim $200,000 in physical damages, and then gave McDonald's a right hook to the jaw by assessing $2.7 million in punitive damages. One of the jurors said he came to realize the case was about "callous disregard for the safety of the people." The punitive damages were later reduced to $640,000 and then to $500,000, but the case illuminates why an apology with an offer of reparation may be a much more effective strategy.[158]

The label Mortification in Benoit's Image Repair Typology may seem to require an over-wrought feeling of remorse. Not so. You can construct a partial apology using any combination of the eight components of a full apology listed above. A partial apology can serve a reputation manager well by expressing regret and sympathy, thereby deescalating a situation without accepting responsibility. Partial apologies—nuanced with admissions of a brand feeling upset, frustrated, or even distraught over an incident—do not have to be worded as full-throated mortification. In fact, communication studies have judged sympathy and compensation language to be just as effective as full apologies.[159]

Time is not our friend inside the Tick-Tock Box, and apologies are "particularly complex." Given those characteristics and assuming you've chosen to include mortification in your messaging, wouldn't it be nice to have a cheat sheet to help decide the best way to apologize? I call the tool I use when it is needed the Mortification Matrix.

IF YOUR PRIMARY GOAL IS...	AND YOUR MOTIVE IS...	...THEN USE THIS APOLOGY TYPE...	...WITH THESE ELEMENTS...	...AND THESE METHOD OPTIONS...	...TIMED FOR BEST IMPACT.
To restore goodwill and trust	To salvage a relationship or absolve embar-rassment	Recovery apology	Full apology (all eight elements)	In person By phone In writing In public	After corrective action is underway. Start fixing the problem first.
To open a path toward reconciliation and favorable resolution, restore civility	To contain or defuse an escalating crisis	Transactional apology	Partial apology (a proportional combination of the eight elements)		After emotions have settled (too soon appears too self-serving).
To set a standard of good behavior and prompt reciprocation by the offended party	To demonstrate alignment with social expectations of good conduct	Principled apology	Full or partial apology		After both parties realize an apology is due. After the offended party is ready to accept it. Before it's obviously too late.

Writing and delivering a good apology isn't easy. Assuming you don't want to find yourself in the same position as lloyd's taco truck, I highly recommend Edwin Battistella's book *Sorry About That: The Language of Public Apology* as a study resource. Battistella provides dozens of examples of notable apologies in recent history.[160]

We don't have to search too hard or too far for contemporary examples. A few years ago, Southwest Airlines stranded millions of travelers during the holidays. Flight cancellations began when severe winter storms swept across the US. Over the span of ten days, the airline cancelled 16,900 flights.[161]

The financial toll was significant: Southwest reported losing approximately $825 million due to flight cancellations and fines imposed by the Department of Transportation.[162]

We can all understand that this was a bad situation brought on by an uncontrollable event. Southwest wasn't the only carrier affected...until it was. Other airlines were able to quickly recover when the weather cleared. Southwest's outdated scheduling system, SkySolver, and their unique point-to-point route network left thousands of flight crew members scattered across the US with no way to connect them to the company's airplanes.

Most airline systems operate in a spider-web-like pattern—a central hub with flights leaving and returning. Southwest, however, operates more like a string of Christmas lights. Crew members move from city to city in a sequence. If one bulb breaks, the rest of the strand stops working. A storm in one city doesn't just affect that one airport; it affects all connecting flights.[163]

Over two million passengers, flight attendants, and pilots were stuck in airports around the country, without luggage, and without the help of customer service representatives.[164]

What would I have said if I was repping Southwest Airlines at the time? Given the situation and the sheer volume of negative news coverage, I would have moved quickly toward Corrective Action and Mortification.

In this situation, Southwest needed to repeat over and over how they were helping passengers and working as hard as possible to fix their system. Their primary messaging needed to be on getting people to where they were supposed to be, no matter the cost to restore civility.

What did Southwest do? Here's what the CEO of Southwest Airlines, Bob Jordan, said during an interview with *Good Morning America*:

This was just an unprecedented storm, for everybody, for all airlines...

The storm had an impact, but we had impacts beyond the storm that obviously impacted Southwest very differently... This is something that we have really never seen in our fifty-one years. We're making investments in our operational areas like always, there'll be lessons learned from this... We're offering refunds, covering expenses—we'll be going back out with even more after that... Beyond safety, there is no greater focus at this point than taking care of our customers, reuniting them with their bags, getting refunds processed. In fact, we've got a special website that's put up just to take refund information...and process that even faster... Our desire is to go above and beyond. We always take care of our customers, that's our fifty-one-year history here at Southwest Airlines. We'll be looking at and taking care of things like rental cars, hotel rooms, meals, booking customers on other airlines—that will all be part of what we're covering as we reimburse our customers and make good on this issue... This has impacted so many people, so many customers, over the holidays. It's impacted our employees, and I'm extremely sorry for that. There's just no way, almost, to apologize enough, because we love our customers, we love our people, and we really impacted their plans... There will be a lot of lessons learned in terms of what we can do to make sure that this never happens again, because this needs to never happen again.[165]

Was this a good apology?
We can score it using the full apology checklist:

1. Statement of remorse? CHECK
2. Account or description of events? CHECK
3. Acknowledgment of the harm or damage caused? CHECK
4. Offer of reparation? CHECK
5. Explicit statement of responsibility? CHECK
6. Request for forgiveness? NOT EXPLICITLY
7. Self-castigation (admitting shame or embarrassment)? CHECK
8. Promise not to repeat the offense by getting better/being better? CHECK

Southwest Airlines grade: a solid seven out of eight. This appears to be a strong apology. Did it work?

Unfortunately, when people miss family holiday gatherings, once-in-a-lifetime reunions, or expensive, nonrefundable vacations, a CEO's apology can't fix everything. While Bob Jordan's words checked most of the boxes, emotions were running too high for the apology to help in the moment. That said, can you imagine the fallout had he not tried?

MESSAGING IN SOUND BITES

In *The Attention Economy*, authors Davenport and Beck say, "Today, attention is the real currency in business and individuals. Understanding and managing attention is now the single most important determinant of business success."[166] The attention span is shrinking, as is the average length of a sound bite. Surely that is not a coincidence, but a reflection of the times we live in. So, when developing a complex message with an apology, we have to remember the audience won't pay attention too long.

Jeff Ansell addresses this subject via a method he calls the "Problem Solution formula." Here's what Ansell says: "the Problem Solution formula is a structured response that joins the problem and solution in one sentence. The first clause or phrase identifies and frames the problem; the second clause offers a solution to that problem. By combining the two components in one sentence, the statement is much more likely to survive the media editing process intact."[167]

This is a smart approach because surviving the media's slice-and-dice editing process is challenging. Message triads, previously introduced in the corrective actions section of our discussion of Image Repair Typology, are also very effective in maintaining attention.

Like any audience, reporters want to hear the beginning, middle, and end of a story. They perceive triads as complete ideas and will hesitate to interrupt their complete delivery. Craft messages in triads and set them up like this: "Three issues are in play as we speak," or "Three findings came out of our investigation..." then count them off. To set the hook, introduce each element of your triad with the phrase, "First and foremost," and then make your first point. Continue with "Second..." and state your second point, and then finish with "Finally..." to stick the landing using the third message in your triad.

As mentioned previously, triads are wonderful messaging tools, which is why it's a mystery that brands fail to use them, especially in complex situations where synthesis is needed. In this context, Chipotle has had me scratching my head on occasion, so an in-depth assessment of their messaging work over the course of a series of food contamination crisis events is in order.

SUPER STORM CHIPOTLE, OR HOW TO LOSE $730 MILLION IN SIX MONTHS

Between 2015 and 2016, Chipotle Mexican Grill was blasted by a ten-episode super storm that cost the company an estimated $730 million.

Let's start by giving Chipotle credit. For many years, the restaurant chain rode the reputation sine wave up with little interruption. It recognized consumer interest in locally grown, locally sourced, naturally cultivated, antibiotic-free food and went on an amazing expansion run. The brand was embraced by millions of consumers and reinforced on a regular basis in interviews. In a 2013 interview, for example, Chipotle spokesperson Chris Arnold said, "Chipotle is probably more transparent about the ingredients we use than any other national restaurant company. We have never professed to being perfect. Rather, the commitment we have made is to constant improvement, and we are always working to find better, more sustainable sources for all of the ingredients we use."[168]

Chipotle's philosophy inspired the company to release a series of short, animated commercials, the first of which was titled "Back to the Start." With background music performed by Willie Nelson, this ad depicted a farmer's journey toward, then away from, industrialized production.[169] On the same theme, Chipotle released its second commercial, "The Scarecrow," which follows the story of a scarecrow who rebels against his job at an industrial food producer. The ad encourages customers to download a video game app that rewards them with a free Chipotle burrito if they rescue all the animals shown in the commercial.[170]

Consumers acclaimed both ads for their creativity and impact, and they elevated Chipotle's brand awareness. With its strapline "food with integrity," Chipotle secured its image as a place to go for a healthy and planet-loving meal. It was great positioning in the exceptionally competitive quick-serve restaurant business, and it set a high bar many other national chains quickly tried to emulate by overhauling menus and remodeling stores.[171]

For the brand, the sine wave crashed down. After several reported outbreaks of E. coli, salmonella, and norovirus at various locations across the country, the chain has been overwhelmed with negative press. With negative press came a significant drop in sales and stock. Ten months after Chipotle's first-reported food-safety incident, Chipotle reported an 82 percent drop in profits. In 2016, *Fortune* magazine wrote, "Popular food chain Chipotle has had a rough year, to put it lightly...Needless to say, the company was in need of massive damage control."[172]

Organizations are often caught flat-footed by unexpected events, primarily because prepping for a bad-news break requires reflecting on what could go wrong, which is an exercise that feels too painful or speculative. The mere act of acknowledging that a product, process, or a public event could result in damage or loss of life is difficult to deal with in the abstract, so thorough preparation is often left unattended.

We can, however, build stronger messaging and put messages in a better sequence to help us face the headwinds of a food safety crisis when it occurs. How well did Chipotle respond? Several news events listed below provide a data set through which we can examine the question.

EVENT #1:

July 25, 2015—Seattle and King County public health officials confirmed an E. coli outbreak, which sickened five people, hospitalizing two.[173]

Chipotle messaging:

None found. Public health officials did not yet connect the illnesses to Chipotle, but this was a precursor that would begin publicly unfolding three months hence.

EVENT #2:

September 10, 2015—Salmonella outbreak in Minnesota.[174]

Chipotle messaging:

"'Since being contacted by the Minnesota Department of Health regarding a possible connection to this issue, we have offered our full cooperation to assist in their investigation, and replaced our entire supply of the suspect ingredient in Minnesota to ensure that it continues to be safe to eat in our restaurants,' [Chipotle Communications Director Chris] Arnold added. 'While this issue in Minnesota does not present an ongoing risk to consumers, we are committed to working with health department officials while they look to determine a cause.'"[175]

EVENT #3:

September 17–October 16, 2015—Bad tomatoes in Minnesota.

Chipotle messaging:

In response, Chipotle removed the offending tomatoes from its Minnesota restaurants and switched to another supplier. *Food*

Safety News invited both the FDA and Chipotle to comment on the progress of the trace-back investigation, but neither accepted the offer.[176]

EVENT #4:

October 31–November 3, 2015—Chipotle closes forty-three restaurants in Washington and Oregon.[177]

Chipotle messaging:

"Chris Arnold, Chipotle's communications director, said in a statement that the people who got sick ate at six different Chipotle restaurants. 'The safety and wellbeing of our customers is always our highest priority,' he said. 'We offer our deepest sympathies to those who have been affected by this situation.'"[178]

After being notified by health department officials in the Seattle (Wash.) and Portland, Ore. areas that they were investigating approximately twenty cases of E. coli, including people who ate at six of our restaurants in those areas, "we immediately closed all of our restaurants in the area out of an abundance of caution."

Chipotle press release: "On the heels of an E. coli incident that was linked to eight of its restaurants in Oregon and Washington state, Chipotle Mexican Grill has taken a number of immediate steps to assist investigators."[179]

EVENT #5:

November 20, 2015—CDC reports E. coli in New York, California, and Ohio linked to Chipotle.

Chipotle messaging:

"'At the moment, we do not believe that it is necessary to close any restaurants,' Chipotle spokesman Chris Arnold said in an email. He said the company has taken measures including deep cleaning in restaurants, replacing ingredients and providing supply chain data to investigators."[180]

Chipotle press release:

- "Chipotle Mexican Grill continues to work closely with state and federal health officials, as the investigation continues into an E. coli incident initially linked to eleven Chipotle restaurants in Washington and Oregon. In response to this incident, Chipotle has taken aggressive steps to make sure its restaurants are as safe as possible."
- "We take this incident very seriously because the safety of our food and wellbeing of our customers is always our highest priority," said Steve Ells, chairman and co-CEO of Chipotle. "We are committed to taking any and all necessary actions to make sure our food is as safe as possible, and we are working diligently with the health agencies."
- "We offer our sincerest apologies to those who have been affected," said Ells. "We will leave no stone unturned to ensure the safety of our food—from enhancing the safety and quality assurance program for all of our fresh produce suppliers, to examining all of our food safety procedures from farm to restaurant, and expanding testing programs for produce, meat and dairy items before they are sent to our restaurants."[181]

EVENT #6:

December 4, 2015—E. coli in Illinois, Maryland, and Pennsylvania. Chipotle messaging/Chipotle press release:

- "(Chipotle)...has taken aggressive actions to implement industry-leading food safety and food handling practices in all of its restaurants and throughout its supply chain. Its enhanced food safety program will establish Chipotle at the forefront of food safety protocols in the restaurant industry... Thousands of food sample tests from Chipotle restaurants linked to the incident have shown no E. coli. No ingredients that are likely to have been connected to this incident remain in Chipotle's restaurants or in its supply system. No Chipotle employees have been identified as having E. coli since this incident began."

- "When I opened the first Chipotle twenty-two years ago, I offered a focused menu of just a few things made with fresh ingredients and prepared using classic cooking techniques," said Steve Ells, chairman and co-CEO of Chipotle. "We do the same thing today, even with nearly 2,000 restaurants, and we are working harder than ever to ensure that our food is safe and delicious."[182]
- "In testing for pathogens, in many ways you're looking for needles in haystacks. Through this high-resolution testing program, we are making the haystacks smaller by working with smaller lots," the company said.[183]
- "Chris Arnold, a spokesman for Chipotle Mexican Grill Inc., said the company's local produce suppliers may not all be able to meet the new standards. The company noted that its local produce program accounts for a 'relatively small percentage' of the produce it uses and only runs from around June through October in most parts of the country."[184]

EVENT #7:

December 9–10, 2015—Norovirus confirmed in Boston Chipotle outbreak, 120 sick.

Chipotle messaging:

In an email, Chipotle spokesman Chris Arnold wrote, "We offer our sincerest apologies to people who were impacted by this incident."[185]

Chipotle CEO Steve Ells appeared on *The Today Show* to apologize:

It's a really tough time. But first I have to say I'm sorry for the people who got sick. They're having a tough time, and I feel terrible about that, and we're doing a lot to rectify this and to make sure this doesn't happen again... With the norovirus, probably, you've heard that this is the extent of it, but it's a disease that is very easily passed and so it spreads very, very quickly from person to person... When we re-open, the [Boston] restaurant will be completely sanitized, and every single employee will have been tested and assured that they do not have norovirus... We've had teams looking at this. We closed our restaurants out of an abundance of caution and tested all the ingredients, surfaces, thousands and thousands of tests back, and they all came back negative for E. coli, and so if there's a silver lining in this, it is that we have looked at every single ingredient that we use at Chipotle... It has caused us to put in place practices that our epidemiologist expert...says will put us ten to fifteen years ahead of industry norms. And I believe this will be the safest restaurant to eat at.

When asked about the potential financial repercussions, Ells responded, "That's not what we're thinking about now. We're thinking about the safety and quality of our ingredients to put in place practices that will not enable this to happen again, practices that are so far above industry norms today that we will be the safest place to eat."[186]

EVENT #8:

December 22, 2015—Chipotle E. coli outbreak spreads to Kansas, Oklahoma, and North Dakota.

Chipotle messaging:

None of the ingredients in our restaurants today were present at the time of these illnesses...

Officials at the Centers for Disease Control and Prevention have indicated that additional cases from similar time periods may still be reported as they make their way through various state health departments to the federal health officials.[187]

If there is a silver lining in this, it's that we've looked at every ingredient. It has caused us to put in place practices that our epidemiologist expert says will put us ten to fifteen years ahead of industry norms.[188]

EVENT #9:

January 8, 2016—US Department of Justice criminal inquiry into Simi Valley, California, norovirus outbreak.

Chipotle messaging:

Chipotle spokesperson, Chris Arnold, declined to discuss most aspects of the probe, but the company said the subpoena covers only the 'isolated' Simi Valley case. "A spokesman for Chipotle said the company plans to cooperate with the investigation as it moves forward."[189]

EVENT #10:

February 2, 2016—CDC declares E. Coli outbreak over.

Chipotle messaging:

"'We are pleased that the CDC has concluded its investigation, and we have offered our full cooperation throughout,' Chris Arnold, a spokesman for Chipotle, said in a statement. 'Over the past few months, we have taken significant steps to improve the safety of all of the food we serve, and we are confident that the changes we have made mean that every item on our menu is delicious and safe.'"[190]

Steve Ells—founder, chairman, and co-CEO of Chipotle—said:

The Centers for Disease Control and Prevention has now concluded its investigation into the recent E. coli incidents associated with Chipotle. We are pleased to have this behind us and can place our full energies to implementing our enhanced food safety plan that will establish Chipotle as an industry leader in food safety. We are extremely focused on executing this program, which designs layers of redundancy and enhanced safety measures to reduce the food safety risk to a level as near to zero as is possible. By adding these programs to an already strong and proven food culture, we strongly believe that we can establish Chipotle as a leader in food safety just as we have become a leader in our quest for the very best ingredients we can find.[191]

What do you think about Chipotle's messaging? We often downgrade brands in crisis when they lack message consistency. That didn't appear to me to be a problem. Chipotle was generally fixed on Corrective Action with transactional Mortification mixed in.

At one point—you can see it in Event #6—a hint of scapegoating showed up when the spokesperson said, "…local produce suppliers may not all be able to meet the new standards." That's interesting, isn't it?

I don't fault Chipotle for establishing Corrective Action as its primary narrative. The challenge I see is that Corrective Action, along with Reduce Offensiveness and Mortification are blame-accepting techniques. When you set an accept-blame narrative, it's difficult to backtrack to Denial or Evade Responsibility messaging.

Further, this series of outbreaks represented an existential threat to the brand, so decisions about messaging quite likely orbited tightly around a "we just need to fix this" mentality. Dissonance-causing pressure from outside voices probably didn't help. This CNBC article excerpt illustrates the point:

"Under previous management, the brand quickly issued 'Buy One, Get One' coupons following food safety scares to help protect traffic, which did not prove successful," Andrew Charles, a Cowen analyst, wrote in a research note Tuesday. "We would like to see CEO Brian Niccol take a more accountable and responsible approach and grab the bull by the horns to clarify what happened, what was remedied, and what changes going forward to limit the risk an event like this will occur again."[192]

Wall Street was almost forcing a Corrective Action approach, wasn't it? It makes sense. Corrective Action has a shiny object quality to it as it tries to vault from inside a crisis to a new future. The Ells quotes about how the events were causing the company to put in place practices that put them ten to fifteen years ahead of industry norms demonstrate this.

It makes me wonder what would have been different if Chipotle had not moved all the way down the Image Repair flowchart to Corrective Action so quickly. Could it have defended itself more skillfully? Consider, in response to the Minnesota salmonella outbreak, rather than Corrective Action, a statement like this:

> The locally sourced vegetables we purchased in Hennepin County appear to have been contaminated by improper cultivation techniques. Our customers expect us to serve the highest-integrity, freshest food, and we expect the same from our producers.

You might be offended by the scapegoating happening here, but isn't it a brand's responsibility to defend its image and reputation? In the context of what would become a $730 million loss in valuation, I suggest only that this ought to be a possibility. Here is another option that may have been used in response to the Boston college students' incident:

> This is obviously upsetting to everyone involved, but unfortunately, Chipotle has no information about where or what the students ate before coming to our restaurants. These factors certainly have to be investigated.

Too slick? Too dismissive? It's a subjective call. It is instructive to wonder, however, if Chipotle either failed to consider other messaging options or intentionally chose not to use them to respond to their super storm.

It took two long years of significant losses for Chipotle to regain its market position. In April 2017, the company reported its first positive sales figures following the events detailed above.[193] Could Chipotle have weathered this storm more easily or helped it pass more quickly if it had put a greater variety of messaging tactics to use? It's not possible to know, but it is essential for students of crisis communications to ask the question.

CHAPTER 9

MESSENGER

"Nobody likes the man who brings bad news."

—SOPHOCLES, *ANTIGONE*

Astronomer is a data platforms company. In normal times, not many people would know about or have heard about the company. I'll talk more about them in Chapter 11, but for this chapter, it's enough to say that the company experienced a reputation crisis when its CEO and Chief People Officer were caught canoodling on a kiss cam at a Coldplay concert. None of the actions taken by these two affected Astronomer's operations or customers; the incident was purely a total and complete embarrassment of two senior people, both married to other people, behaving badly in a public setting. In the wake of the incident, the CEO resigned, and performative statements were issued by the company and the CEO. I thought Astronomer's subsequent messenger selection was a stroke of brilliance.

The company hired Gwyneth Paltrow, the ex-wife of Coldplay's lead singer, Chris Martin, to rep it by spoofing what had happened. Paltrow identified herself as the company's "temporary spokesperson" and addressed the internet's most intensive questions. One read, "OMG! What the actual f..." Her response was, "Yes, Astronomer is the best place to run Apache Airflow. Unifying the experience of running data, ML, and AI pipelines at scale. We've been thrilled so many people have a newfound interest in data workflow automation." The sendup goes on for a few more questions and showed us all how a ridiculous situation can be cleverly side-tracked with an appropriately ridiculous response. What makes the piece effective is we know Paltrow has little-to-no idea what Astronomer is or what it does. She is a pitchman, a "very temporary spokesperson," as she put it.[194]

As good as Astronomer's response was, the messenger in the Rapid Response Model isn't a pitchperson, but an authentic ambassador with a professional stake in the brand's reputation and success. When bad news breaks, messengers take on a heavy responsibility. Selecting the right spokesperson for a brand can mean the difference between successfully concluding a crisis, versus prolonging it. Inside the Tick-Tock Box, you don't get much time to do this. The assumption is made that a rapid response team is equipped with competent professionals with more than one being capable of facing reporters and stakeholders during a crisis. The question is, which member of the RRT is the right one to choose?

Shouldn't it automatically be the CEO? Eric Dezenhall says, "The main criterion for a strong leader in crisis situations is a capacity for making decisions."[195] I agree, but we're not necessarily talking about the leader of an organization, who may not be a spokesperson for the brand. Besides, Dezenhall argues that the organization's leader has to retain the capacity and the thinking bandwidth to manage the dissonance of a situation. That's absolutely right. The time may come when the chief decision-maker on the rapid response team—whether the CEO, president, or executive director—becomes the spokesperson, but it shouldn't be assumed as the default. If that's true, then who is the right person?

This is a tricky question, because when the leader assumes the role of spokesperson, it is often a point of no return. Once the press and public have access to them, they will be less than satisfied to hear from staff or other representatives.

I thought I had found some guidance on this question in materials from the Centers for Disease Control and Prevention. One of its publications states: "It's difficult to capture all qualities of a good spokesperson and pass them on to others but it's not difficult to identify the qualities of a poor spokesperson."[196] And then it goes on to say...ummm...nothing else. Okay, let's keep looking.

What do others in the field say about the specific criteria we should use to select a spokesperson? Having read three books by media-training experts—one of whom claims to have the world's most-visited media-training website—I'm surprised to have found no answer to this question. These sources are chock-full of advice on how a spokesperson should perform, but all assume the right individual has been selected for the role.[197]

Others have offered a wide range of advice. Choose someone with the right personality, the right expertise, or solid communication skills, they say. Pick someone with confidence and a positive personality, or someone who looks professional, organized, and put together. Select a person who can "demonstrate sincerity and transparency during an interview...[while also being able] to determine the fine line between empathy and apology if need be."

I came across some useful advice from Alan Hilburg, president and chief executive of the crisis management firm, Hilburg-Malan. When asked whether and when a CEO should be used as a spokesperson, he said there are three questions to ask:

1. Has the scope and scale of the issue been elevated to where it could adversely affect brand trust?
2. Has the integrity of executive decision-making been called into question?
3. Is the genesis of the crisis values-created?

If the answer to any of these questions is yes, Hilburg believes the CEO should be the spokesperson.[198] I like Hilburg's reasoning, but the questions he asks are related to the character of a brand and the people who support it. They're integrity oriented, which makes sense. But character, especially in crisis work, where corrective action is called into play, has a companion: competency. The character/competency relationship has to be acknowledged. It is what trips up spokespeople, because while they may be well-equipped to address one dimension, they are likely to be lost when both are in play.

Where does this leave us? Is a public relations person the right spokesperson? What about the board chair, the CEO, president, or a subject-matter expert? The frustrating answer to these questions seems to be "it depends." Of course, this is too ambiguous to be of any help, so, we need a model.

In the matrix below, I've combined character and competency with a third variable, Chandler's Classic Crisis Stages (see Introduction) to create a 3x3 tool.

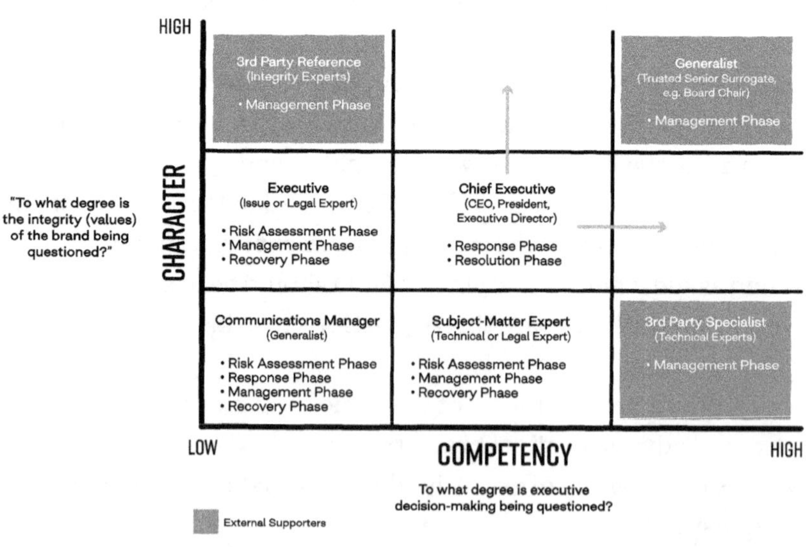

Because we're in the Tick-Tock Box, we can't forget the importance of time, so like the other models in the latticework, I've designed the Messenger Selection 3x3 for quick decision-making. To use it well, just ask three questions:

1. On a scale from low to high, to what extent is the *character* of our brand being questioned, attacked, or at risk? Character attacks, also known as ad hominem attacks, are those "in which an argument is rejected, or advanced, based on a personal characteristic of an individual rather than on reasons for or against the claim itself."[199] Use a simple "high/medium/low" grading scale to help find an acceptable plot point on the axis.

2. On a scale from low to high, to what extent is the *competency* of our brand being questioned, attacked, or at risk? Again, use a simple "high/medium/low" grading scale to help find an acceptable plot point on the axis.

3. Where are we in time? If the Warning phase in Chandler's Classic Crisis Stages model has passed and a bad-news break has occurred, the answers to the previous questions may not be clear. If that's the case, you're likely in the Risk Assessment or early-Response stage, so use your communication manager—the person serving as the rapid response team's spokesperson. Recall from the earlier chapter: The communication manager's responsibility is to shield key leaders from a barrage of inbound questions, so they can focus on incident management.

As dissonance builds, a rapid response team's chief decision-maker may conclude the severity of character and competency attacks require escalating to a different spokesperson. If character issues are most in play, an executive with general expertise about an issue would be a good choice, as would an executive who is adept at public-facing communications due to temperament, talent, or training. This person should be credible, believable, and able to demonstrate a genuine interest in the well-being of the affected stakeholders. On the other hand, if competency is under attack, roll out a technical expert to blunt competency-threatening criticism. Note in the matrix that a brand's legal counsel can be effective in either role if they possess that temperament, talent, and training.

When to use a chief executive? When the character or competency of the brand, or both, are under a sufficient threat. Only good judgment can dictate the precise timing, but it seems most useful to have a chief executive serve as spokesperson during the Response and Resolution stages.

The general strategy for addressing a brand crisis can be framed during the Response phase, and the chief executive can own this better than any other character in the Messenger Selection Matrix. It's natural to link strategy to outcome, so moving the chief executive to the forefront to address crisis resolution is smart and aligns with stakeholder expectations.[200]

Per Chandler's Classic Crisis Stages model, the acme of a crisis occurs in the Management phase. If it is determined that additional voices are needed to support the brand's reputation, then move to the top-left, top-right, or bottom-right cells in the 3x3. These cells represent the domain of preachers, politicians, and professors.

Find nonprofit executives (preachers) who have benefited from your company's philanthropy to speak publicly in favor of your brand. Swing former government regulators who know your track record or supportive elected officials (politicians) into action if they are trusted allies. On the competency axis, technical experts—such as health officials, epidemiologists, or other credentialed professionals (the professors)—can be great voices to put into play. Combine them to form blue-ribbon panels to strengthen their individual voices.

The added advantage of using outside experts is their ability to slow down the clock. The public almost always allows a respected technical expert or panel time to carefully assess an issue before rendering a judgment. Be aware, however, that stakeholders tolerate technical experts who become hired guns on behalf of a brand for only so long. Credibility comes from detachment, objectivity, and deliberate speed. If a blue-ribbon panel takes too long to render its views, its own competency comes under scrutiny.

At the height of a crisis, a generalist may be brought in if events escalate to a point where the chief executive's continued employment is in peril. For public companies and even large private ones, board chairs have primary fiduciary responsibility, so crafting messaging that extends to all affected stakeholders is essential.

Inside the Tick-Tock Box, you were given just a few minutes to choose your messenger. It's not fair, is it? I get it. All I can suggest is taking some encouragement from Shakespeare, who said, "I like not fair terms and a villain's mind."[201]

We are in a crisis, so we have to embrace the unfairness of the situation, hope your rapid response team has an array of capable messengers, and move forward to confront the next challenge: preparing your messenger to face the public...likely through interaction with the media.

Anheuser-Busch faced this choice when it found itself in a firestorm of controversy from which it is still recovering after partnering its Bud Light brand with transgender influencer Dylan Mulvaney. Though the partnership was a one-off gesture celebrating Mulvaney's 365-day milestone of womanhood, the collaboration generated severe backlash.[202] Conservative celebrities like Kid Rock launched public boycotts, and conservative media used the incident to decry how even the world of beer had gone "woke."[203] Within a week of the promotion, sales dropped by 26 percent compared to the same period in the previous year. Bud Light lost its position as America's number one best-selling beer and saw its market value decline by over $ 40 billion.[204] The company has still not regained 30 percent of the customers lost during the backlash.[205]

To contain the damage, Anheuser-Busch's CEO, Brendan

Whitworth, was thrust into the messenger role. He issued a public statement on the company's website, saying:

> As the CEO of a company founded in America's heartland more than 165 years ago, I am responsible for ensuring every consumer feels proud of the beer we brew. We have thousands of partners, millions of fans and a proud history supporting our communities, military, first responders, sports fans and hard-working Americans everywhere. We never intended to be part of a discussion that divides people. We are in the business of bringing people together over a beer. My time serving this country taught me the importance of accountability and the values upon which America was founded: freedom, hard work and respect for one another. As CEO of Anheuser-Busch, I am focused on building and protecting our remarkable history and heritage. Moving forward, I will continue to work tirelessly to bring great beers to consumers across our nation.

Whitworth's statement was widely criticized for being a disaster and a nothing statement. *Forbes* writer Paul Tassi called it: "Honestly one of the worst corporate statements I've ever read. Just 100% air."[206]

It's okay to hate the statement's words, but I would argue that the bigger issue was that Whitworth should never have been the spokesperson to begin with. He was pulled into the middle of a highly polarized cultural conflict that had little to do with a CEO. His presence didn't resonate with either side, and due to his neutrality, many members of the LGBTQ+ community felt that Anheuser-Busch abandoned its support for them.

Who would've been a better messenger?

When looking at the messenger selection model, this is a high-character, low-competency situation. The better messenger for this situation would likely have been a third party. My choice? Kid Rock and Dylan Mulvaney.

Imagine a series of ads featuring Dylan Mulvaney and Kid

Rock. They could attack the issue at hand in a humorous way, for example, by pranking on each other through hilarious contrivances that ultimately bring them together over a Bud Light. As unlikely as this idea sounds (see Astronomer and Paltrow to get into the right frame of mind), a large-enough budget makes almost anything possible. The episodes could have reframed the crisis by creating a space for connection rather than division. This bold move could make a ridiculous situation more ridiculous, bleed off the negative emotions, and put the brand back on its feet (it's not too late, by the way!).

The important lesson from this is that the messenger matters just as much as the message, and you have options. The CEO isn't always the best choice. The right messenger is a person who resonates with the audience and can redirect the conversation away from the negativity.

Remember when the cybersecurity company CrowdStrike released a faulty software update that caused millions of Microsoft Windows computers to crash, and left users with a blue screen? Airlines, banks, hospitals, media outlets, and hotels all suffered a significant financial blow as they could not access core computing systems.[207]

CrowdStrike moved quickly. Within seventy-nine minutes, they contained the issue and began remediation efforts.[208] In less than two hours, CrowdStrike's CEO, George Kurtz, posted a public statement on the company's website saying:

Valued Customers and Partners,

I want to sincerely apologize directly to all of you for the outage. All of CrowdStrike understands the gravity and impact of the situation. We quickly identified the issue and deployed a fix, allowing us to focus diligently on restoring customer systems as our highest priority.

The outage was caused by a defect found in a Falcon content update for Windows hosts. Mac and Linux hosts are not impacted. This was not a cyberattack.

We are working closely with impacted customers and partners to ensure that all systems are restored, so you can deliver the services your customers rely on.

CrowdStrike is operating normally, and this issue does not affect our Falcon platform systems. There is no impact to any protection if the Falcon sensor is installed. Falcon Complete and Falcon OverWatch services are not disrupted.

We will provide continuous updates through our Support Portal.

We have mobilized all of CrowdStrike to help you and your teams. If you have questions or need additional support, please reach out to your CrowdStrike representative or Technical Support.

We know that adversaries and bad actors will try to exploit events like this. I encourage everyone to remain vigilant and ensure that you're engaging with official CrowdStrike representatives. Our blog and technical support will continue to be the official channels for the latest updates.

Nothing is more important to me than the trust and confidence that our customers and partners have put into CrowdStrike. As we resolve this incident, you have my commitment to provide full transparency on how this occurred and steps we're taking to prevent anything like this from happening again.[209]

Why was Kurtz the best spokesperson to lead the crisis response? The answer lies in the fact that the crisis involved both character and competency attack points. In that capacity, and understanding the factors at hand, he delivered timely and consistent updates across multiple platforms. Within the first twenty-four hours, he issued a recovery apology, posted regular updates on social media, and participated in two national broadcast interviews. Although many end users may not have recognized him by name, Kurtz made a deliberate effort to increase visibility and establish a reassuring presence.

Even so, the problems escalated. Company IT departments had to manually repair every affected computer, and in many cases, it took days to get systems fully restored. Recognizing they could not physically intervene at scale, CrowdStrike created step-by-step video tutorials and published detailed written guides to support users and help speed up recovery.[210]

To amplify their reach and increase awareness, CrowdStrike partnered with Microsoft as a trusted and widely recognized third-party messenger. Microsoft clarified the source of the disruption. Its communications guided confused users, deflected blame, and redirected traffic to CrowdStrike's recovery resources.[211]

The combination of internal authority and external credibility underscored the value of using multiple messengers in a crisis. By pairing direct leadership from within the company with the voice of a familiar partner, CrowdStrike strengthened its ability to clarify the situation and reach audiences more than a single spokesperson would have.

CHAPTER 10

MESSENGER PREPARATION

"Don't only practice your art but force your way into its secrets; art deserves that, for it and knowledge can raise man to the Divine."

—LUDWIG VAN BEETHOVEN

This chapter confronts three obnoxious realities: the existence of sound bites, the disappearing existence of media relationships, and the effect of news syndication at scale.

REALITY #1: THE 8.95-SECOND SOUND BITE

Reputation managers know actual crises are often made worse by perceptions. We also know social and media reports, especially in the midst of crises, are often riddled with inaccuracies. The biggest insider secret not even the media may realize about its behavior is the way stories are edited to match a stakeholder's attention span. The average length of a sound bite reveals the evidence.[212]

Daniel Hallin, a professor at the University of California, San Diego, conducted a study regarding the length of sound bites in the media. He used a stopwatch to time the length of sound bites in twenty weekday-evening news broadcasts during each presidential election year from 1972 through 1984, and twenty-five weekday-evening news broadcasts during each presidential election year from the two endpoints of the study, 1968 and 1988. His samples were taken from September and October of each year, using footage from each major television news network. What did he find? A steady decline in the length of sound bites.

In 1968, the average length was 43.1 seconds; in 1972, 25.4 seconds; in 1976, 18.2 seconds; in 1980, 12.2 seconds; in 1984, 9.9 seconds; and in 1988, 8.9 seconds. He summarized the results by stating, "The truth is that one-liners and symbolic visuals are what get on the air."[213]

Between 2012 and 2014, I was curious to see if Hallin's 8.9-second finding remained consistent when the medium shifted from video to print. Over the course of those two years, my staff and I built a database containing 2,841 quotes—946 from the *Houston Chronicle*, 945 from *The Dallas Morning News*, and 950 from the *Austin American-Statesman*—harvested from the first story on the front page of the print edition of each paper. Using a words-per-minute rate of 167—the cadence established as average by researcher Emma Rodero in her benchmark of English-speaking radio broadcasters—I did a quick mathematical conversion of the print quotes to sound-bite lengths.[214] Guess what we found? Bingo! The average length of a sound bite in print equaled 8.95 seconds of talk time.

My study, done decades post-Hallin yet still remarkably consistent with his results, tells us the media has dialed in on a viewer's attention span. And while the 2015 Microsoft "Attention Span of a Goldfish" study (reportedly twelve seconds) has been generally debunked, for our purposes, it's enough to agree attention span creates a default toward peripheral processing, making communicating about a reputation-damaging event all the more difficult.[215]

If the fact that we're living in an age where the average length of a sound bite is 8.95 seconds isn't frustrating enough, the rise of robot reporters will really jack up your blood pressure.

REALITY #2: THE END OF MEDIA RELATIONS

The phrase "media relations" is rapidly becoming anachronistic. In my crisis communication experience, reporters I thought I had built great relationships with turned on me as soon as they smelled blood. In my early days, this caught me off guard. It also set up an adversarial mindset about reporters I still harbor today. But a few years ago, I found research that helped create a new perspective.

In a thirteen-year study, more than four hundred journalists were asked their views regarding relationships with PR practitioners. The results showed fewer than half viewed their relationships with practitioners as positive, and 18 percent viewed them as "necessary evils." The study surfaced an interesting finding: Although journalists may say relationships with practitioners are important, they put responsibility for relationship-building squarely on PR practitioners. What's more, the study discovered attitudes toward PR practitioners only improved "during times of news-editorial staff cutbacks."[216]

One of the reasons this phenomenon—the decline of media relationships—is accelerating is because journalism has been invaded by algorithm-based robot reporters going by names like Wordsmith, Quakebot, Heliograf, BuzzBot, Wibbitz, and News Tracer, among others.[217]

Robot reporters are increasingly used by news organizations to create the content in newsfeeds. Tens of thousands of news articles appearing every day are scraped from content on the web and assembled by these natural-language programs that, ironically, were created by traditional media outlets, such as the Associated Press, the *Los Angeles Times*, and *The Washington Post*. Relationships with reporters matter less today because robots are replacing qualified journalists and, unlike people, they don't go to lunch. Kristian Hammond, co-founder and chief scientist for a company called Narrative Science, once predicted that more than 90 percent of news will soon be written by algorithms.[218]

The effects are already apparent. From 2008 to 2018, newsroom employment in the US dropped by 47 percent, from about 71,000 workers to 38,000.[219] Reporters, editors, photographers, and videographers in newspaper, radio, broadcast television, cable, and digital news services have all taken a hit. Digital-native news sites aren't immune, either. Several years ago, BuzzFeed News laid off a hundred people and even the once-popular Vice Media is defunct.[220]

It's okay to feel a little empathy for reporters. They work under deadline pressure and constantly face the threat of being replaced by a robot, so they don't have the time or latitude to become experts on a subject. They're worried about their jobs, and they're not in the market for friends, especially when covering fast-moving crisis events.

REALITY #3: MASSIVE SYNDICATION

Formulaic news used to be less visible to viewers, but for years, Conan O'Brien made it his mission to expose television news outlets that not only report the same stories but also use identical scripts. In a periodic segment, O'Brien featured clips of TV anchors and reporters from stations across the country committing this copy-and-paste sin.

If you want to see some hilarious and somewhat depressing examples of how syndication has taken over the news, search the web for "Conan, Local News Recycling." The search results will give you a glimpse of a few videos where the phenomenon of syndication is on full display. *The Washington Post* reporter Paul Farhi explained the syndication phenomenon: "Stations not only get prepackaged footage from such services, but a script that introduces the footage, as well." It may feel journalistically shoddy, but it's financially irresistible. Marc Jaromin, president of Stratus Content Partners, an Iowa-based news outsourcer, estimates stations using syndicated content save 80 percent of the cost of producing a traditional all-local newscast.

The Adweek blog site TVSpy featured an O'Brien bit showing twenty-five anchors introducing a story about ice cream with the words, "I scream, you scream...well, you know the rest."[221] Similarly, a YouTube video compilation entitled "Mindless Media" shows eighteen news anchors setting up a consumer news story with the line, "Economic factors may take some spring out of the Easter Bunny's step this year."[222] In another hilarious piece, O'Brien lampoons twenty-three local television news affiliates asking the same question to introduce a story called "Is It Time For Dogs To Have A Social Network Of Their Own?" and wraps up the bit with, "That's depressing."[223]

SmithGeiger, a consulting firm serving television stations, even has a story carousel website targeting newsroom producers. The Quick Turn Story Ideas blog is designed "to feed your special reports calendar in the coming weeks" and lists a range of stories, including roads needing repair, dangerous drive-by restaurant delivery people, smartphone radiation, and the use of LSD to treat post-traumatic stress disorder.

Deborah Potter, executive director of NewsLab, a broadcast training and research center, provides further evidence of the trend: ABC, CBS, NBC, and Fox each have about two hundred affiliates, and CNN Newsource provides content to more than one thousand stations. Potter says, "Like the networks, CNN makes it easy for local stations to run these stories by providing scripted introductions for local anchors to read, and read them they do, even when they don't make much sense." The insatiable need for broadcast, web, and mobile content by television news has turned syndicated content into a necessity and has converted journalists—particularly anchors—from reporters to script readers whose primary value is to "perform" the news, using their personalities to create viewer allegiance.[224]

Journalist-turned-author David Henderson went straight to the bottom line of the issue: "Far too many of today's television anchors are nothing more than actors or readers with no journalistic training or credentials."[225] Media analyst Andrew Tyndall provides support for the assertion, saying, "With the exception of the usual intro and sign-off segments, television news anchors have been relegated to very specific, nearly superfluous tasks for very specific amounts of time." Tyndall's research boiled the anchor's job down to these segments: 140 seconds introducing reports from the field, 140 seconds of voiceover reading, 120 seconds in intro and sign-off, and an occasional live report from the field.[226] He found that evening news anchors average four minutes of face time and seven minutes of speaking time nightly.[227]

The newspaper industry has embraced syndication for decades. Just as newspaper syndicators have consolidated in an effort to reduce costs, broadcast syndicators are following their lead. United Media, which began as the Scripps syndication service, folded into Kansas City-based Universal Uclick, ending a 109-year run.[228] What caused the end of a century-old syndication provider? The perpetrator seems to be "the changing needs of newspapers and media companies in the digital era where space is tight, budgets are tighter, and time isn't the luxury it once was."[229]

The use of pool reporters and wire services is a long-practiced method in the newspaper world. *The Boston Globe*'s Globe Services Newsroom even had a Q&A on the subject that read, "Question: Does The Globe use material from other sources? Answer: *Globe* staff is limited in number and can't be everywhere, so some stories and photos in the *Globe* are taken from wire services, such as AP or Reuters." Although the syndication model for newspapers is not new, the pressure on newspaper balance sheets may force news reporters to conform, subconsciously, to a storytelling schema similar to what television anchors are required to read every night.

Six media giants now control 90 percent of what we read, watch, or listen to—down from fifty companies in 1983. Just 232 media executives control the information diet of 277 million Americans, and the big six media outlets in 2012—GE, News Corp, Disney, Viacom, Time Warner, and CBS—control 70 percent of cable content. News Corp owns the top newspaper on three continents; Clear Channel owns twelve hundred radio stations; and 80 percent of radio stations' playlists are identical.[230]

All this means messengers need to quickly convey a complex set of ideas and emotions to an audience to set a narrative and a directional orientation toward normal, and it must be crafted in a format robot reporters can scrape, and outlets can easily syndicate. The first step is shaping the best possible message using the tools from the previous chapters and crafting them using Ansell's Problem Solution sound bite formula. The next step is to prepare for media interviews by guessing what a reporter might ask and be ready with an array of possible responses.

Do we really have to just guess? Former *USA Today* reporter Sally Stewart tried to help when she said, "What reporters really want is usually pretty simple: they want their call returned, they want a quote for their story, and they want to do their jobs and go home."[231]

That's not much help, honestly. After a few dozen more hours of conversation with former reporters about the question, a research question formed around the idea of making more than a guess about what a reporter might ask. Could we find a pattern that predicts what they might ask? This question meant diving deep into the skeletal system of the media interview to look for patterns.

Others have worked to map this terrain. J.L. Vance, a former FBI agent, suggested media interviewing is made up of seven steps:

1. Define the issue.
2. Gather facts and prepare organizational messages.
3. Brainstorm potential questions.
4. Answer the questions in writing.
5. Rehearse out loud.

6. Set ground rules during the callback, such as the time, length, and site of the interview, as well as related matters.
7. Conduct the interview.[232]

Isabel Wilkerson, a former reporter, offered her seven-step list for how a media interview works:

1. Introduction
2. Adjustment—the "feeling-each-other-out" phase
3. Moment of connection
4. Settling-in phase
5. Revelation—when a source is feeling "comfortable enough to reveal something very candid or deep"
6. Deceleration—the winding down of the interview, signified by the closing of the reporter's notebook
7. Reinvigoration—when a source "feels free to say almost anything, and they make a revelation or comment that could be the very best quote of the interview."[233]

Vance's seven steps don't even mention the interview itself until the final step, while Wilkerson's entire list serves to warn potential interviewees of the knuckleball tactics reporters use to get sources to swing wildly at gut-spilling questions. As with Messages and Messengers, it's obvious we need a model.

THE PREDICTIVE INTERVIEWING MODEL (PIM)

After two years of research, transcribing 505 radio interviews, and statistically analyzing 2,112 questions asked by reporters, the tool I have been searching for has arrived. I call it the Predictive Interviewing Model (PIM), which my team now uses to train hundreds of participants nationwide every year.

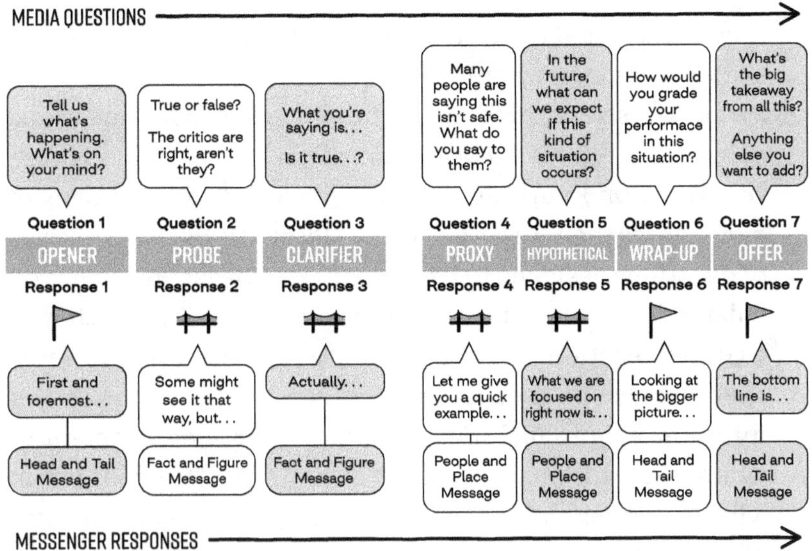

The first thing to know about the PIM is interviewers ask six question types. The second is they ask these six question types in a statistically predictable sequence. The bottom line: Interviews, like Vonnegut's story model (see Messaging chapter), have a shape to them, and the Predictive Interviewing Model maps it.

TOP HALF OF THE PREDICTIVE INTERVIEWING MODEL

For easier reference, each step of a media interview is labeled horizontally in the center of the PIM. The first question in every interview: "Can you say and spell your name for me and tell me your title?" This is administrative, so it isn't included in the model, but once it has been asked, the interview begins.

- Opener Questions. Statistically speaking, interviews start with an open-ended question that casts a wide net to allow a source to set up the "act, scene, and agents" of a story.[234] The PIM gives an example of this question type and others across the top of the model. Open-ended questions may include interrogatives associated with "the three key W's of the story: the who, the what, and the where."[235]

- Probe Questions. Probes are difficult-to-answer questions, sometimes referred to as "gotcha" questions. White House reporter Ron Fournier once described his use of probes in questioning then-Texas Governor George W. Bush as "a series of questions designed to trip him up, or at least knock him off balance."[236] Probe questions are constructed by eliciting an irritated reaction or embarrassing an interviewee. However, they can also be used in a closed-ended fashion to goad an interviewee into making an on-the-record commitment or guarantee. This may be done by asking them "to choose from a list of answer choices."[237] Probes may be posed in the form of double-barreled questions, defined as those in which "opinions about two objects are joined together so that respondents must answer two questions with one answer."[238] Probes may sometimes be crafted as leading questions designed to "subtly prompt the respondent to answer in a particular way."[239] They sound like this: "Sir, do you know how fast you were driving?" Asking a question raises the prospect that a problem exists.
- Clarifier Questions. Clarifying questions do not require an interviewee to formulate an opinion before responding; instead, they ask for a specific fact, comparison, or list of information.
- Proxy Questions. Proxy questions use faceless sources (e.g., many people or everyone) to create the impression of investigative reporting and the illusion of knowing the bigger picture. Statements like, "I've spoken to many people who..." or "Many are upset over this..." are red flags that a proxy is on its way. Proxy questions are posed with a common- or prior-knowledge slant, as if the reporter has already interviewed or extensively researched a subject and, therefore, legitimately represents an audience to an interviewee. This has been referred to as a "strategy of reliance on faceless (secret) sources" and a way to "efficiently create an image of inves-

tigative reporting, even though no legitimate reasons for its use could be found."[240] Another study characterized proxy questioning as an information-gathering method associated with prisoner-interrogation techniques, where interviewers provide "opportunities [for a source] to add information and confirm or disconfirm claims," creating "the illusion of knowing it all."[241]

- Hypothetical Questions. Hypothetical questions ask an interviewee to speculate about the disposition of a topic, using a temporal shift. They can be formulated as, "What might happen if...?" or "Six months from now, will we be in the same situation we find ourselves in today?" They can also be phrased as unipolar questions, where the respondent is asked their opinion about a future scenario in isolation from others, or as bipolar questions, where the source may be asked to "choose between two contrasting objects; for example, "Do you think the government should adopt a graduated income tax rate in the future or do you favor changing to a flat-rate income tax?"[242]

- Wrap-Up Questions. Wrap-ups are not unique types of questions. They play an important function in the PIM, though, as they are typically either opener or probe questions, restated differently to indicate an interview is about to close. Be aware that rhetorical questions—those "asked without the expectation of an answer...posed for dramatic effect, [or] to drive home a point" may also be used inside the wrap-up to provide a signal that the interview is ending.[243]

- Offer Questions. The offer question is almost always the final question in a media interview and phrased as, "Anything we haven't covered?" or "Is there anything else you would like to add?" Offers are nearly always extended but rarely aired or seen. Interestingly, reporters believe the technique "almost universally results in the source providing the best quote."[244] This means the function of an offer is different from its counterparts. Instead of serving as a true interrogative, its primary purpose is to provide a last opportunity in the interview for a quote to be delivered. It's the reason veteran newsroom editors start by listening to or viewing an interview clip at the end of an interview.

Other types of questions may have come to mind as you read through the descriptions above. Closed-ended questions, for example, are typically probes. Leading questions can be characterized as probes, clarifiers, proxies, or hypotheticals. It's not difficult to imagine listing dozens of types of questions, but the utility of doing so runs out quickly. The primary types identified in our research have proven to be statistically reliable when modeled.

BOTTOM HALF OF THE PIM

With the types of questions and probable sequence of asking them known, it's much easier to prepare a messenger for interactions with the media or other stakeholders. Anticipating incident-specific questions is a best practice in crisis communication. It's also an exercise that can be done before a bad-news break occurs when you're not operating in the fog. But even if preparation work hasn't been done, the PIM helps you focus on the few questions most important to address.

Books by media trainers are filled with thousands of dos and don'ts regarding how a messenger should perform during an interview. None are wrong. Unfortunately, they're almost always too abstract to be useful: "be transparent," "remain calm and responsive," and—one of my favorites—"trust yourself during the interview." I don't know what these mean, honestly, and inside the Tick-Tock Box, we don't have time to ponder their intent. Instead, the bottom half of the PIM provides three rhetorical tricks for messengers to use.

The first trick is this: Respond, don't answer. Think of an interview as an interactive performance or presentation, not as a soul-baring tell-all or legal deposition. You are not under oath. However, you have a duty to represent your brand in a way that protects its reputation. Use sound bites to deliver the ideas your stakeholders need to hear, especially in the Question 1/Response 1, and Question 7/Response 7 steps.

The second trick—and as noted by the icon in the Response 1, 6, and 7 blocks—use flags to control message delivery. A flag emphasizes a priority, focuses attention on a key message, and strengthens message discipline. Good flags sound like this:

- "First and foremost..."
- "The main point I want to stress is..."
- "Our primary concern at this moment is..."
- "The most important thing your viewers should understand is..."
- "At the end of the day, everyone needs to keep in mind..."
- "The bottom line here is..."

The best messengers take full advantage of the Question 1/ Response 1, and Question 7/Response 7 steps to drive home the key idea to protect a brand's reputation.

The third and final trick—also indicated in the PIM by the icons in the blocks for Responses 2 through 5—use bridges to pivot out of harshly worded questions designed to paint you into a corner. Effective spokespeople use bridges like these:

- "Some people believe that, but another way to look at it is..."
- "I've heard that said, and there is some truth to it, however..."
- "Actually..."
- "The fact is..."
- "What we're hearing from people is different..."
- "What concerns me more is..."
- "I don't know, but what I do know is..."
- "It's too early to respond to that. Our focus right now is..."
  (Special note: This bridge is terrific when you're asked a jerky

question like, "Do you want to take this opportunity to apologize?" or "Do you expect a lawsuit over this?").

Since this book isn't designed to be a media training guide, other devices, such as head-and-tail messages, fact-and-figure messages, people-and-place messages, nonverbals, impression-making, background selection, stance, off-the-record messages, nonattribution, no comments, and other important concepts aren't addressed. Keep in mind that messenger preparation inside the Tick-Tock Box should focus on developing responses to a few key questions. The PIM tees these up and reduces the ambiguity created when the prospect of facing the media or difficult stakeholders arises. It's an excellent life preserver in a storm.

It's important to reinforce the sequence for addressing bad news. Research from Brigham Young University tells us when receiving bad news, most people prefer directness, candor, and very little buffer, if any.[245] This confirms Daniel Pink's advice, and we're reminded that breaking bad news first in the sequence of the interview is better than waiting. Take advantage of this by positioning your first message up against the opener question in the PIM.

One note for specificity: Interviews aren't completed inside the Tick-Tock Box. Determine whether an interview should be considered at all by stepping through the next model: the Methods of Outreach 2x2.

CHAPTER 11

METHODS OF OUTREACH

"Mother considered a press conference on a par with a visit to a cage of cobras."

—Margaret Truman

Marshall McLuhan once famously declared, "The medium is the message."[246] One of the most intriguing crises—Blue Bell Creameries's 2015 listeria outbreak—provides both a factual review and a counterfactual straw man to test McLuhan's maxim.

On April 20, 2015, a video featuring the CEO of Blue Bell Creameries, Paul W. Kruse, was posted on YouTube.[247] It's a short piece, only thirty-two seconds long, but it's remarkable for a number of reasons. A transcript helps set up the analysis to come:

We are heartbroken over this situation and apologize to all of our loyal Blue Bell fans and customers. Our entire history has been dedicated to making the very best and highest quality we possibly could, and we're committed to fixing the problem. Ice cream is a joy and a pleasure to eat, it certainly is for me, and I do it every day, and it should never be a cause for concern, and for that we do apologize, and we're going to get it right.

I scratch my head every time I watch that video. Ice cream is a joy? What events led to this? Why did Blue Bell's CEO feel two apologies in one statement were necessary? Why was the word "heartbroken" used without context? Who was the intended audience, and how did they react? Why was video the right choice as a method of delivery? Was it effective? The latter two questions are the focus of this chapter, but to make sense of Blue Bell's choices, a bigger picture is needed.

We'll back up for just a moment and then address the previous questions. Blue Bell Creameries is located in Brenham, Texas, a small town with a population of about fifteen thousand people. The creamery is one of Brenham's major employers. For more than a century, Blue Bell's ice cream and frozen snack products have been a favorite in home freezers, especially in Texas and across the South. In television ads, the brand portrayed its creamery as an idyllic place where happy cows nuzzled up to little girls in sun dresses and bonnets running barefoot through pastures festooned with wildflowers. Purity, innocence, and happiness were all balled up together. One series of particularly schmaltzy ads regaled Blue Bell in song as "the best ice cream in the country."[248] Perhaps even more than Chipotle, Blue Bell seemed beyond reproach—the brand enjoyed an enormously loyal following for decades. That changed when a cascade of bad news hit the company. Here's how events unfolded:

February 12, 2015. The South Carolina Department of Health and Environmental Control found listeria as part of a routine sampling of two Blue Bell single-serving ice cream products (the Chocolate Chip Country Sandwich and the Great Divide Bar) and traced them back to Blue Bell's creamery in Brenham.[249]

On February 13, the FDA and South Carolina officials notified Blue Bell of the findings. Subsequently, the Texas Department of State Health Services collected samples of the same two products at the Brenham creamery. Its tests found the same listeria isolates as were found in South Carolina, and listeria was found in another ice cream product, called "Scoops," made on the same production line.[250] Neither the FDA nor state regulators insisted on public disclosure, reasoning that the only products then known to contain listeria were single-serving items, which are usually sold to institutions and convenience stores, so they would be easily retrieved. Under no obligation to do so, Blue Bell chose not to announce publicly that it had sold tainted ice cream.[251]

March 13, 2015. The FDA announced listeria-contaminated frozen treats were linked to three deaths and five illnesses in people who ate Blue Bell products at Via Christi Hospital St. Francis in Wichita, Kansas.[252] The FDA warned consumers not to eat ten types of novelty products made by Blue Bell and pulled the products from store shelves and hospitals. The same day, Blue Bell issued its first recall in 108 years, removing ten products made on the same production line from the market.[253] It also shut down the production line in question at its Brenham facility and posted this statement on its website:

> One of our machines produced a limited amount of frozen snacks with a potential Listeria problem.
>
> When this was detected, all products produced by this machine were withdrawn. Our Blue Bell team members recovered all involved products in stores and storage.
>
> This withdrawal in no way includes our half gallons, quarts, pints, cups, three-gallon ice cream or take-home frozen snack novelties.[254]

Also on March 13, Kruse interviewed with *The Wichita Eagle*, saying:

> They feel that this one production line we use here is what might have caused the problem. It's a complicated piece of machinery, it's been down for about a month and a half, and what we're likely going to do

with it is throw it out the window, so to speak so we know how to do it right. And now we have to look at what happened here.[255]

Kruse was also quoted in a March 13 *Houston Chronicle* story as saying the machine used to make Scoops and other single-serve items had not been in operation for about a month and a half, putting its shutdown well before South Carolina's February 12 discovery of listeria.[256]

March 22, 2015. The Kansas Department of Health and Environment reported listeria had been isolated in Blue Bell single-serving, three-ounce institutional/food service chocolate ice cream cups collected from Via St. Christi, the same Kansas hospital involved in the outbreak.[257] Samples of Blue Bell brand three-ounce institutional/food service chocolate ice cream cups collected from the company's Broken Arrow, Oklahoma, facility also yielded listeria.[258] This meant the bacteria were active in two plants separated by 475 miles.

In a press release, Blue Bell indicated it was "working closely" with officials "in order to resolve this issue," but continued emphasizing the problem was limited to "select stores and food service accounts."[259]

March 23, 2015. Blue Bell expanded the recall to include three flavors of three-ounce institutional/food service ice cream cups with tab lids produced at its Broken Arrow facility.[260] The company recalled three products identified as contaminated, plus seven others manufactured on the same line in Brenham, from twenty-three US states. "This recall in no way includes Blue Bell half gallons, quarts, pints, cups, three-gallon ice cream or the majority of take-home frozen snack novelties," the announcement added.[261]

In a press release on March 23, Blue Bell acknowledged the connection between its products and the Wichita outbreak and expressed regret. Blue Bell also provided consumers with UPC numbers to identify the recalled products, and a phone number to call with questions, but the phone line was only answered Monday–

Friday, 8:00 a.m. to 5:00 p.m. CEO Kruse conveyed the company's regrets for its part in the illnesses and deaths.[262]

In a statement on Blue Bell's website, Kruse said the contaminated ice cream cup was made in Broken Arrow on April 15, 2014. "This recall in no way includes Blue Bell Ice Cream half gallons, pints, quarts, three gallons or other three ounce cups."[263] A March 25 news story reported Kruse saying, "We are devastated and know that Blue Bell has to be and can be better than this. Quality and safety have always been our top priorities. We are deeply saddened and concerned for all those who have been affected."[264]

March 27, 2015. Kruse issued a public apology to consumers and retail customers via an open letter. There was no mention of listeria, or of the illnesses and deaths in the Wichita hospital.[265] Excerpts from the letter are captured below.

- "I want to personally apologize for any anxiety or inconvenience caused by recent recalls of certain Blue Bell products..."
- Kruse pointed out he realized the event created "concern" for consumers, "who for more than a century, have come to trust us to provide quality ice cream products."
- Kruse explained the company was completing an internal investigation and "ceased production on the lines where the recalled product was made."
- For the second time, Kruse indicated, "Everyone at Blue Bell regrets this incident" and "are deeply saddened and concerned for all who have been affected."
- Kruse reassured customers the company is "working tirelessly to make sure that we provide a safe product."
- Kruse thanked consumers and retail customers whom Blue Bell had "served for generations for their patience, understanding, and loyalty during this difficult period. Nothing is more important to us than maintaining your trust. All of us at Blue Bell hope you will give us the opportunity to continue to serve you."[266]

April 3, 2015. The CDC linked Blue Bell to ten listeriosis cases in five states and recommended that consumers not eat, and institutions and retailers not serve, any products made at the company's Oklahoma facility, in addition to any previously recalled or withdrawn products. The FDA released inspection reports showing the company had found the bacteria in its Oklahoma plant on surfaces, such as floors and catwalks, on seventeen occasions, beginning in March 2013.[267] On April 3, 2015, Blue Bell Creameries issued a statement they had voluntarily suspended operations at their facility in Oklahoma, saying:

> Blue Bell Creameries is voluntarily suspending operations at our manufacturing plant in Broken Arrow, Oklahoma. We will then thoroughly inspect the facility for any possible problems that may have led to the contamination of some of our ice cream products in the past few weeks. We are taking this step out of an abundance of caution to ensure that we are doing everything possible to provide our consumers with safe products and to preserve the trust we have built with them and their families for more than a century.[268]

The suspension would allow a "team of experts" to "conduct a careful and complete examination to determine the exact cause of the contamination," the statement said.[269] "We apologize in advance for any inconvenience this step may cause, but we believe it is the right thing to do for you, our consumers, who for generations have relied on Blue Bell for the freshest and finest ice cream."[270]

April 6, 2015. The CDC recommended consumers "not eat products" produced at the Broken Arrow facility. Walmart, Kroger, and Sam's Club took Blue Bell products out of their freezer aisles.[271]

April 7, 2015. The FDA notified Blue Bell one of the samples it had collected in its joint inspection with Oklahoma health officials, a pint of Banana Pudding ice cream, had tested positive for listeria. Blue Bell announced a third product recall, including ice cream and sherbet pints and half-gallons made at Broken Arrow from February 12 through March 27, 2015.[272]

April 8, 2015. The CDC reported that whole-genome sequencing confirmed three of the four isolates from people in Texas were nearly identical to listeria strains isolated from ice cream produced at Blue Bell Creameries's Oklahoma facility. These three people were added to the case count for the outbreak, bringing the total to eight.[273]

April 20, 2015. Blue Bell issued a voluntary recall of all its products made at all of its facilities—including ice cream, frozen yogurt, sherbet, and frozen snacks—and halted all production. The action covered twenty-three states and the international market. The recall covered an estimated eight million gallons of ice cream, frozen yogurt, sherbet, and frozen snacks.[274]

The company issued a press release with the headline: "Blue Bell Creameries voluntarily expands recall to include all of its products due to possible health risk." The news release said Blue Bell was recalling all its products "because they have the potential to be contaminated with *Listeria monocytogenes,* an organism which can cause serious and sometimes fatal infections in young children, frail or elderly people, and others with weakened immune systems."[275]

The press release issued on Blue Bell's behalf distributed by the FDA, stated:

Today's decision was the result of findings from an enhanced sampling program initiated by Blue Bell which revealed that Chocolate Chip Cookie Dough Ice Cream half gallons produced on March 17, 2015, and March 27, 2015, contained the bacteria. This means Blue Bell has now had several positive tests for Listeria in different places and plants and as previously reported five patients were treated in Kansas and three in Texas after testing positive for *Listeria monocytogenes.*[276]

In the same statement, Blue Bell said it planned to implement a "test and hold" procedure for all products at its manufacturing facilities, meaning every Blue Bell product would be tested for contamination and released only after being proven safe. The company said it also would expand the cleaning and sanitizing of its equipment, send samples daily to a microbiology lab for testing, and provide additional training to employees. Further, Blue Bell said it would resume distribution of its ice cream "on a limited basis once it is confident in the safety of its product."[277]

April 21, 2015. The CDC reported whole-genome sequencing confirmed that people from Arizona (1) and Oklahoma (1) were part of the outbreak, bringing the total case count to ten.[278]

April 24, 2015. Blue Bell halted production at all facilities and announced via press release plans for an intensive cleaning and retraining program.

Meanwhile, posts by fans on Blue Bell's social media pages evidenced strong customer support. Its Facebook page began seeing comments such as, "Still the best ice cream in the country and well worth however long we have to wait." In response to several comments, Blue Bell expressed appreciation and said, "We're working hard to be back soon." Supportive advertisements stating "God Bless Blue Bell" appeared in the *Houston Chronicle* and were later posted on Blue Bell's Facebook fan page.

April 27, 2015. Blue Bell issued a press release vowing to make a fresh start. Kruse stated, "We intend to make a fresh start and that begins with an intensive cleaning and enhanced training."[279]

April 28, 2015. Blue Bell released a statement saying that floor repairs and potential work on ventilation systems at Blue Bell ice cream plants would be part of an intensive maintenance overhaul that could take months to complete. That same day, health inspectors found listeria at Blue Bell's Sylacauga, Alabama, plant.[280]

In the statement, Blue Bell Vice President of Operations Greg Bridges said, "We are committed to doing whatever it takes to get this right. Our manufacturing facilities, especially the two in Brenham, are large and complex, so we expect this process will take some time."[281]

May 7, 2015. In response to a Freedom of Information Act request by the *Houston Chronicle* and other news outlets, federal regulators released documents showing Blue Bell knew about bacteria problems in its plants as early as 2013 but failed to correct them. The FDA findings raised troubling new questions, including why—given that Blue Bell knew listeria was in its Oklahoma plant for years—the company didn't shut down operations as soon as listeria turned up in ice cream this year. Blue Bell's incremental recalls and public statements initially suggested listeria was limited to a single production line.[282]

The company issued a press release quoting Kruse and detailing the status of each manufacturing plant and the steps being taken to respond to FDA inspection findings. He indicated "we do not yet have a firm timeline" for returning to stores, but "we believe at this time that it will be several months at a minimum." He explained, further, that production and distribution would only begin when "we can do so with confidence" and stated the company was creating "the cleanest, safest environment possible to produce the high-quality, great-tasting ice cream that people expect from Blue Bell."[283]

The same day, Blue Bell spokesperson Joe Robinson sent an email to the *Houston Chronicle*, stating:

Several swab tests did show the presence of Listeria on non-food surfaces in Blue Bell's Broken Arrow (Oklahoma) plant in 2013. As is standard procedure for any such positive results, the company would immediately clean the surfaces and swab until the tests were negative. We thought our cleaning process took care of any problems, but in hindsight, it was not adequate, which is why we are currently conducting such a comprehensive re-evaluation of all our operations.[284]

In a separate statement, company officials said they were preparing detailed responses to the FDA findings and reiterated their commitment to conduct extensive plant upgrades, new product testing, and employee training.[285]

May 8, 2015. The FDA released a statement clarifying that the agency was not aware of Blue Bell's listeria findings until performing its first inspection of Blue Bell Creameries in 2015. (Previous inspections were performed by other parties.) "When Listeria is found in the manufacturing environment, rather than on the food itself, it is not uncommon for a company to immediately take corrective action, rather than test further to see if the strain of Listeria poses a threat," the FDA said in a statement. "Although Blue Bell's testing did identify Listeria, the company did not further identify the strain to determine if it was pathogenic. Therefore, it is not known whether the strain found in 2013 was Listeria monocytogenes or another non-pathogenic type of Listeria. The FDA continues to work with the company to ensure that its processes and practices comply with food safety laws and regulations."[286]

May 15, 2015. Blue Bell laid off and furloughed 1,450 of its 3,900 employees—the first job cuts in the company's history—and issued a video statement explaining its actions.[287] The decision came a day after the company announced agreements with Oklahoma and Texas to require notifying state officials whenever a positive test result for listeria in its products or ingredients appeared. "Blue Bell has no firm timeline to begin making ice cream again. The company expects to phase in production over time, and for a year, officials have agreed to hold onto each batch of ice cream until test results for listeria come back negative."[288]

In a May 15 press release and video posted on Blue Bell's website and Facebook page, both entitled "An Agonizing Decision," Kruse stated:

The agonizing decision to lay off hundreds of our great workers and reduce hours and pay for others was the most difficult one I have had to make in my time as Blue Bell's CEO and President. At Blue Bell, our employees are part of our family, and we did everything we could to keep people on our payroll for as long as possible. At the same time, we have an obligation to do what is necessary to bring Blue Bell back and ensure its viability in the future. This is a sad day for all of us at Blue Bell, and for me personally.[289]

Comments on Blue Bell's Facebook page were both critical and supportive. Negative comments indicated Blue Bell's greed and unsanitary conditions caused the layoffs, while many other posts expressed sorrow for the company and cited examples of Blue Bell's previous charitable actions as reasons the public should continue supporting the company. Blue Bell did not respond on its social pages.

May 20, 2015. In response to a request from a Dallas newspaper, the FDA released observations of FDA inspections at Blue Bell Creameries facilities in Brenham, Broken Arrow, Houston, and San Antonio between 2007 and 2014. None of these earlier inspections indicated evidence of listeria contamination; however, numerous violations of food-safety protocols were observed by Texas state health officials, who reportedly did the 2007–2012 inspections under contract with the FDA.[290]

May 22, 2015. In a lengthy letter to the FDA's Dallas district, Blue Bell declared its corrective actions would take longer than expected. The letter was sent in response to the agency's inspection observations issued at its ice cream processing facilities in Brenham and Broken Arrow. The company responded separately to the FDA's New Orleans district regarding its Sylacauga, Alabama, facility.[291]

July 14, 2015. Beset by negative press and delays in isolating the source of the bacteria, a cash-strapped Blue Bell struggled to jumpstart its operations. According to both the *Houston Press* and *The Wall Street Journal*, the crisis had sent Blue Bell's annual revenue plummeting from $680 million in 2014 to $500 million in 2015. In mid-July, Fort Worth billionaire Sid Bass brought Blue Bell back from the brink, shelling out $125 million in a deal that gave him one-third ownership in the company. The infusion of money helped Blue Bell restart production, and by early September, the company began selling its first half-gallons in the Houston and Austin areas, as well as in parts of Alabama.[292]

Citing its privately owned, family-run status, Blue Bell declined to comment publicly on any aspect of Bass's financial involvement in the company. Kruse issued a boilerplate statement: "We are pleased Sid Bass has made a significant investment with our company. The additional capital will ensure the successful return of our ice cream to the market and our loyal customers."[293]

According to *The Wall Street Journal*, the day before—Monday, July 13—Kruse sent a letter to Blue Bell shareholders informing them of Bass's investment, which he said was essential to remain in business. The newspaper said the letter, which it had reviewed, stated Blue Bell had been unable to raise enough capital from existing shareholders to remain operational, so the company's board of directors had opted to "work with a single source" who could provide the necessary financing.[294]

August 5, 2015. Alabama public health officials gave Blue Bell the okay to resume production and sale of ice cream manufactured at its Alabama plant.[295]

August 17, 2015. In a press release and a video posted on its website and social media sites, Blue Bell Vice President of Sales and Marketing Ricky Dickson said Blue Bell is "back doing what we love…making ice cream" and announced its ice cream would return to stores on August 31, 2015, with a limited production capacity. Dickson also explained a five-phase plan in which Blue Bell would return to select markets and expand slowly to fifteen states, down from the previous twenty-three state markets where it had previously been available.[296]

September 1, 2015. Blue Bell restarted production at its Broken Arrow facility.[297]

November 18, 2015. Blue Bell announced via press release it had begun production at its headquarters plant in Brenham. Blue Bell said the plant would not produce ice cream for sale in stores at that time. "Operations are currently on a limited basis as the company seeks to confirm that new procedures, facility enhancements and employee training are effective. Ice cream produced will be closely monitored and tested. There is no firm date for when ice cream from the Brenham facility will be available for sale."[298] The release went on to say, "Blue Bell is currently in phase two of its five-phase return plan and plans to enter phase three on December 14. Austin was in phase one, with the ice cream returning to store shelves on August 1." The company says nearly seven hundred employees who were put on paid furlough earlier in the year had returned to work. The company also posted a thank-you video from Blue Bell employees: "Today, the Blue Bell brand lives on, but recovery may be many more years in the making."[299]

I contacted Blue Bell to ask for an interview about this case and I even sent them a list of questions for review, but I received no response, which is not a surprise. Can you blame them? Who wants to relive this nightmare!?!

Can you imagine the intensity of the dissonance Blue Bell must have been feeling? A clue lies in the volume of media coverage the brand received over the 2015 timeframe. Have a look at the chart below to get a view at what must have felt like a king-sized gut pretzel. Notice on the left end of the graph that from February to March—this would have been close to Blue Bell's "normal"—the brand rarely registered a presence in the news. In fact, in February, Blue Bell was mentioned in the press just eleven times. In April, things snowballed with a jump to 305 mentions. Then May 7 hit—the heaviest single day in the year when 1,253 mentions got recorded—with most mentions associated with the revelations that the brand knew about its listeria problem for some time.

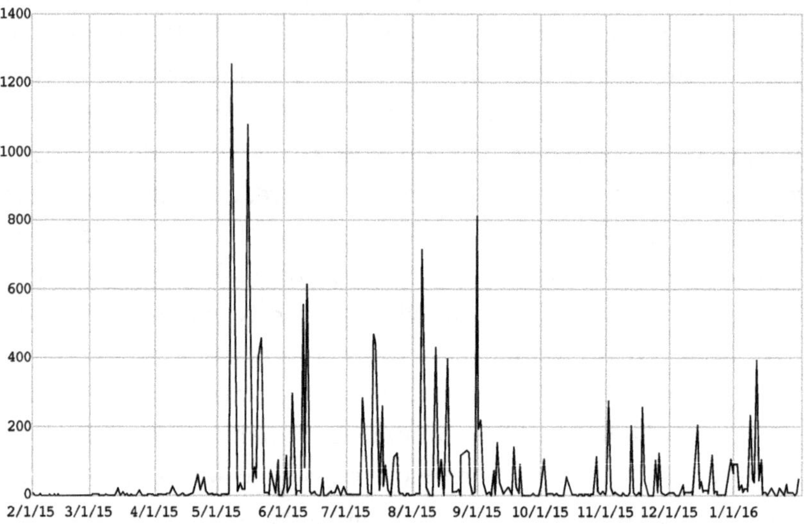

It's interesting to examine Blue Bell's messaging. Most of it swings between Corrective Action and Mortification from an Image Repair standpoint with occasional Reduce Offensiveness techniques mixed in. Likewise, the messenger selection is worth a look. CEO Paul Kruse did most of the heavy lifting, but on occasion, technical managers, a generalist spokesperson, and regulators were pushed into service. In this chapter, though, I used the Blue Bell analysis to explore the question, "How does a brand get the word out?" What options can a brand use to deliver its message to stakeholders who control the narrative of a bad-news break? In the following table, I have used a few examples from the Blue Bell case to begin listing options.

#	DATE	EVENT	METHOD(S) USED
1.	February 12	FDA and South Carolina officials notified Blue Bell of listeria	No public comment
2.	March 13	FDA: Listeria-contamination linked to three deaths and five illnesses	Statement website posting
3.	March 13	First recall in 108-year history	Serial interviews— *The Wichita Eagle*, *Houston Chronicle*
4.	March 22	Kansas Department of Health and Environment reported listeria	Press release
5.	March 23	Acknowledged connection between its products and the Wichita outbreak	Press release and website posting
6.	March 27	Apology from CEO	Open letter

Blue Bell's method selections have a clear pattern of preference toward highly controlled, written statement-making, usually in the form of press releases. Of thirty-seven total messages, only two were delivered via press interview.

The company's preference for press releases is a bit ironic. Just a year before Blue Bell started making ice cream in 1907, the press release was invented by a guy named Ivy Lee to describe the causes and aftermath of train derailment in Atlantic City causing the deaths of more than fifty people.[300] More than a century later, veteran PR executive Frank DeMaria observed, "The press release should have died years ago. In my mind, they're dead already."[301] DeMaria doesn't say it in as many words, but his larger point is that today, brands have an array of options available for delivering messages to stakeholders.

What does this set of selections tell us about Blue Bell? If the medium is the message, does the brand's management harmonize with its image? Maybe. Maybe like its preference for highly controlled communications, it takes a near-obsessive control over cleanliness, safety, and quality to live up to its "the best ice cream in the country" motto. What we can safely say is that a crisis of this magnitude is no place to discover that authentic voice.

The Blue Bell study reminds us that options get overlooked or disregarded when the pressure of dissonance descends on a rapid response team. It also prompts us to figure out what method or methods authentically align to a brand before things go south. Before methods get chosen, though, pause for a moment and ask yourself a crucial question: What audience do we need to reach most?

You're not wrong if you answer "the public," but it's not exactly right, either. Stakeholder theory defines the public as any group that can affect or be affected by the operations of an organization, so it's a big range that could include everyone from government officials to employees to the local community.[302] The trouble is, answering "the public" is too broad and too nebulous to be of much help. Where ambiguity reigns, models can rule. Let's head into a cornfield to talk about a tool you should have in your toolbox. What you'll find is that it has terrific adaptability to the Method question we're trying to answer.

For a few years, my brother, Kevin, made a living building transmissions for race car driver Bobby Allison, one of NASCAR's fifty greatest drivers and a three-time winner of the Daytona 500. Kevin lived in an airplane hangar near Fort Worth, Texas. At one end was a very cool apartment; the rest of the hangar was filled with a mind-boggling array of tools, rolling tool chests, lifts, compressors, welders, plasma cutters, spare parts, you name it.

Along with all the state-of-the art stuff he has, he has some vintage tools, too, including a collection of one-quart glass bottles with metal spouts affixed to their tops. They look a little like gray traffic cones stuck onto the top of mason jars. Kevin inherited them from our Grandpa Ed Stull who used them to store and pour lubricants. I'm the kind of person who thinks about trading in a vehicle when the gas tank gets low, so it's fair to say Kevin and I don't share an affinity or aptitude for fixing mechanical things. But like he has his store-and-pour jars, I have a vintage tool I use when working through stakeholder questions—the Diffusion of Innovations Model made famous by Everett Rogers way back in 1962.

Rogers grew up on a farm outside Carroll, Iowa. His father embraced the electric and mechanical farm innovations of the day but was skeptical of those involving biologics or chemicals. He had heard about a new hybrid seed corn, but he refused to use it, although it was said to yield 25 percent larger, more drought-resistant crops than the seed he'd always used. Then came the drought of 1936, and along with it, the hottest, driest July in 140 years.

While the hybrid seed corn on his neighbor's farm stood healthy and tall in the blistering heat, the Rogers family's crop wilted.[303]

A long, scorching-hot summer will get a person to thinking, and that was obviously the case for Rogers. He was perplexed as to why some farmers—including his own father—had waited so long to use the new hybrid seed corn, even after it became obvious it was better than the old sort in every way. This put him on the path toward finding out what it takes for any idea or product to gain acceptance and momentum enough to spread through a population or social system.

In his book *Diffusion of Innovations*, Rogers described the way an idea spreads or becomes popular as "diffusion."[304] He found some people—innovators—are more willing to accept a new idea or product than others. These are venturesome people who are eager to try new ideas, risk-takers, people who can deal with a high degree of uncertainty. Rogers theorized only about 2.5 percent of the population are innovators. Next are early adopters—respectable people, opinion leaders in their communities who observe the innovators' early experimentation and then join them.

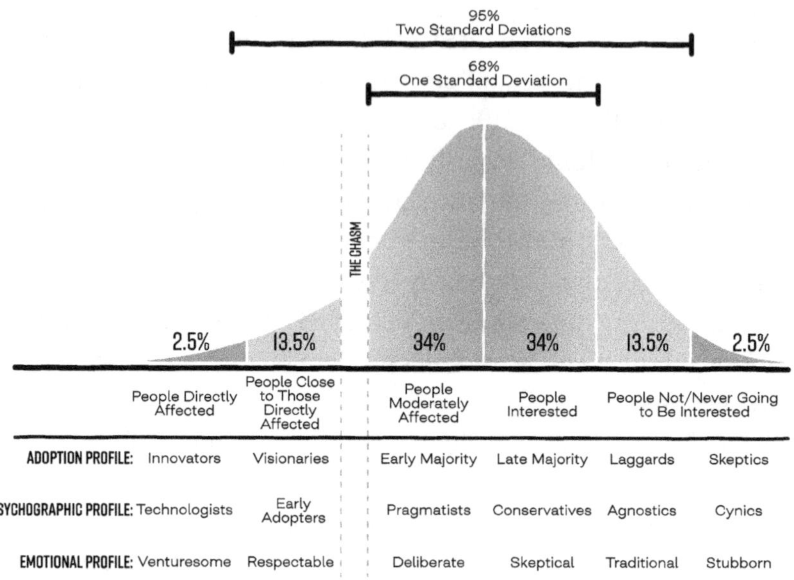

Early adopters account for about 13.5 percent of the population. They are followed by the early majority—a deliberative group of people who think about the innovation quite a while before adopting it. Representing about 34 percent of the population, they don't want to be the first or the last to try something new. They provide connectivity with the next group—the 34 percent of the population who make up the late majority. They're skeptics who usually accept something new because of peer pressure and wait until almost everyone else has opted for it before joining in. Finally, Rogers said, we have the laggards. They are the 16 percent of society who are highly traditional, slow down the change process when they can, and rarely understand why others adopted the idea.[305]

For rapid response team purposes, when a crisis occurs, the innovators, early adopters, early majority, and late majority are the interested stakeholders. The model uses a bell curve to depict the magnitude of the impact on each group, from left to right. Those on the left end of the model are directly affected and deserve special attention. Those in the middle require a still different approach.

And those on the far right may or may not be interested at all, so don't burn energy on them.

Because speed is an overriding concern inside the Tick-Tock Box, focus on the stakeholders in order of priority starting from the left end. Your broad choices include, but certainly are not limited to:

- Employees
- Investors
- Customers
- Suppliers
- Channel partners
- Neighbors and community
- Influencers
- Elected officials
- Government regulators
- Public safety officials

Notice "the public" is not a stakeholder; "neighbors and community" is more descriptive. "The media" is not a stakeholder, either; it is a conduit to your stakeholders, an amplifier of your message to ensure it reaches those you want and need to influence most. Some members of the media are exceptions; if a particular reporter or editor has a track record of setting a narrative and has the power to sway other media outlets to follow, characterize that person as an influencer. Pool reporters or young professionals fresh out of radio, television, and film school are still learning the ropes of being sent alone to cover six events a day, grab a sound bite, and move on. Give them credit for being amplifiers only.

Others have layered additional labels for each of the stages in Rogers's model as they've applied psychographic or emotional viewpoints. I don't know the extent to which these have been tested and proven, but I like some of them, so I've included a few in the diagram—without explanation, as no validating research seems to exist. Still, it's fun to think about each and do your own compare/contrast.[306]

One additional point about the Rogers's model: A critical phase in a crisis is the gap between early adopters to the early majority, which sociologist Morton Grodzins called the "chasm." This is the valley of death for ideas—the point at which messages run out of steam. Grodzins said if early adopters succeed in getting their idea across the chasm and spreading it to the masses on the other side, they've created a "tipping point" after which the curve rises sharply, as the masses accept the idea, and sinks again when only the stragglers remain.[307] Malcolm Gladwell wrote a great book called *The Tipping Point* about this part of the Diffusion of Innovations Model.

When bad news is breaking, Rogers's model reminds us that our messaging and messenger may not be of interest to, or even noticed by, the public as a whole. Instead of trying to reach everyone, then, our real priority is to select a method with which we can create narrative control within a short time, targeting the groups at the left end of the bell curve. We can address other audiences later, but while we're in the Tick-Tock Box, it's smart to confine attention to those most directly affected.

Now that we've determined which stakeholders we need to reach most, the question becomes how do we reach them? The Blue Bell case study provides a starting point, but the company didn't use other obvious options, and like just about every other question in the damnable world of crisis communication, there is a bushel basket of them. Would yet another tool help? I think you know the answer. Here is my Methods of Outreach 2x2 widget.

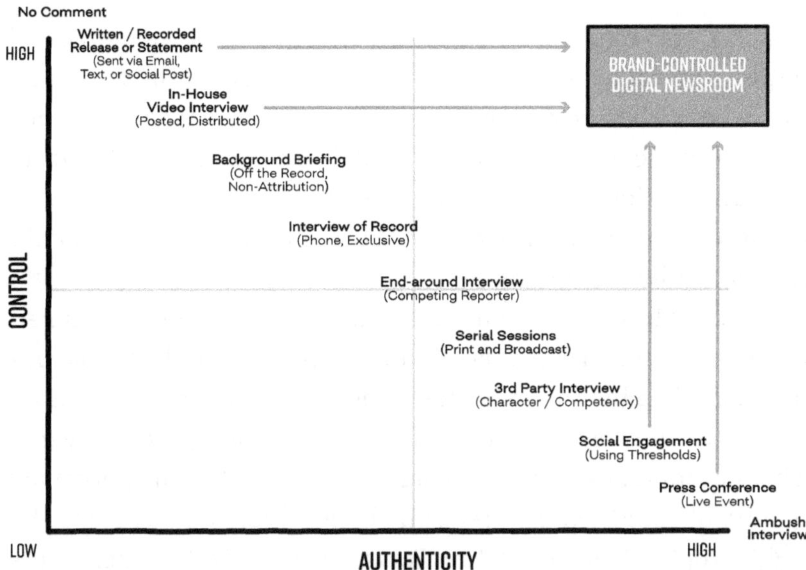

A few quick notes before jumping inside this tool: Individual briefings, sidebar discussions, one-on-one phone calls, and even small-group meetings are options for communicating to essential stakeholders during a crisis. Inside the Tick-Tock Box, we are concerned with reaching the most people within the shortest amount of time, so the options presented are intended for mass distribution. By pushing the variables of control and authenticity against each other, several potential mass distribution methods emerge.

Why choose control and authenticity as the forcing variables? In their book, *The Power of the 2x2 Matrix,* Alex Lowy and Phil Hood talk about 2x2 thinking as a "universal and highly transferable" path to extraordinary ends—an approach to problem-solving that allows a complex situation to be examined in a matrix framework as a set of conflicting interests.[308] I use control against authenticity because they represent conflicting interests. The tension created between the two allows options to materialize and be positioned in an easy-to-grasp pattern.

Like Coombs's Crisis Type Matrix and the Messenger Selection 3x3, this model provides a fast way to evaluate a method of delivery options. The layout provides clarity about the trade-offs involved with each option. It is a comprehensive choice architecture conforming to what Nobel Prize-winning behavioral economist Richard Thaler said: "As the choices become more numerous...good architecture will provide structure, and structure will affect outcomes."[309]

In the Methods of Outreach 2x2, the vertical (Y) axis represents how much control you can exert over the delivery of your message. The higher an option appears on the Y axis, the more control a brand has over the delivery of a message, and vice versa. The horizontal axis (X) represents authenticity—the perceived quality of being genuine, real, and believable. The further to the right an option appears on the X axis, the more likely stakeholders will perceive it as authentic.

"No Comment" is at the top of the option staircase. Conan O'Brien got quoted saying, "People should say 'no comment' more often. No comment! I love 'no comment.' Let's have more 'no comment,'" which was funny, but in crisis communication work, "no comment" is deadly for authenticity. When you hear someone in the news say it, what do you think? They must have something to hide.

After reviewing scores of clients' crisis communication plans, most of them warning never to say "no comment" when briefing the media, I get a feeling that "no comment" is losing its popularity. On the other hand, it is a thing, and it can be said. In the plasma-like world of crisis communication, "never" is too fixed and unnegotiable. In some rare cases, "no comment" may be the best choice. I don't like it, I don't recommend it, but I acknowledge it is an option, so it merits a spot at the top-left corner of the 2x2. Highest control, lowest authenticity.

The "Ambush Interview" at the bottom-right of the option staircase is equally problematic. In an ambush interview, a reporter and camera operator catch an unprepared brand spokesperson off guard—usually in front of an office building or in a parking lot—stick a microphone in their face, and fire questions at them, hoping to get a damning sound bite. Television viewers see this as the ultimate "gotcha" moment. Generally, they regard the ambush interview as highly authentic because the media has set the story up with wild allegations to fit a predetermined narrative.

The ambush interview reminds us why a good crisis plan includes setting up a protected perimeter to allow rapid response teams to come and go from the scene of the incident, unimpeded by rogue reporters. Establishing a media corral at the scene is certainly a best practice to support a smart perimeter strategy. A spokesperson can visit the corral at regular intervals to update reporters, as the situation warrants.

Ambush interviews are an option in the Methods of Outreach 2x2 because spokespeople can choose to participate in them or not. Reporters and their crews cannot legally detain a spokesperson or block their safe passage, and spokespeople don't have to answer questions. Through our Predictive Media Network, our team teaches clients to escape ambush interviews by using lines like these:

- "You caught me on the way to the bathroom…I absolutely have to go now."
- "I'd be happy to help you, but you've caught me going into a meeting. When can I call you?"
- "I appreciate your interest and want to get you the information you need. I've got some people waiting for me. Let's set a time to talk later."
- "I'd like to track down the latest information. What's the best way to contact you?"
- "I don't have that information right here, but we want to help. What's your deadline?"

These lines only work if they're repeated over and over until the reporting crew gets exasperated enough to give up and go away.

By comparing ambush interviews to no-comment responses, you can feel tension inside the 2x2. By pitting control against authenticity, a polarity gets set up and the energized tension between the poles informs us that every option comes with a trade-off.

As with the Coombs Crisis Type Matrix, the Image Repair flowchart, and the Messenger Selection 3x3, the value of the Methods of Outreach 2x2 is not just that the options are quick and easy to evaluate. The model also prevents rapid response teams from knee-jerking a decision to, say, hold a press conference simply because the team is ignorant to the existence of the array of available options. Understanding the value of each option can help bring this point to life, so here's a short explanation for each.

WRITTEN/RECORDED RELEASE OR STATEMENT

The brand creates a written statement and then distributes it to stakeholders or amplifiers, such as the media via email, text, or social media posting.

A brand's website can also be used. The best practice, as shown in the Methods of Outreach 2x2, is to set up a digital newsroom on a brand-controlled website. A digital newsroom provides three significant upsides:

1. It provides a go-to point for reporters away from your normal online brand presence. Time-starved reporters love using digital newsrooms to grab content and brand assets including logos and photos. They're going to find them anyway or use assets you may not like, so set up an easy-to-access (no password required) place for these items to live.

2. It can serve as your one-stop-shop broadcast station where you report your news—yes, this means bad news, too—the way you

want it reported with your key messages leading the way. Why rely on the whims of headline writers motivated only to sell clicks to their readers? Shape your message with your words and bang your drum by distributing the stories you publish to your stakeholders via social media or email.

3. Robots can scrape and may use the content. See the Messenger chapter regarding the robot reporter phenomenon.

If you don't have a digital newsroom, then controlling your message is much more difficult. Once again, Blue Bell provides an example. In July 2019, a fourteen-year-old in Lufkin, Texas, took a half-gallon of Blue Bell's Tin Roof ice cream out of the freezer in a Walmart store, removed the lid, licked the top of the ice cream, put the lid back on, and returned it to the freezer. It was a dumb prank. Even dumber: Her friend recorded the dirty deed on a smartphone and posted the video on social media. Needless to say, things went bad for the fourteen-year-old once the security footage was reviewed and the police found her.

Here's what was weird: Blue Bell made a statement in the form of a pop-up posting at the top of the home page of its website to communicate about the incident. This is what it looked like:

We have identified a Walmart in Lufkin, Texas, as the store where the malicious act of food tampering took place. Our staff recognized the location in the video, and we inspected the freezer case. We found a Tin Roof half gallon that appears to have been compromised. Based on security footage, the location and the inspection of the carton, we believe we may have recovered the half gallon that was tampered with. Out of an abundance of caution, we have also removed all Tin Roof half gallons from that location.

The Lufkin Police Department has been notified and is taking over the investigation.

The safety of our ice cream is our highest priority, and we work hard to maintain the highest level of confidence of our customers. Food tampering is not a joke, and we will not tolerate tampering with our products. We are grateful to the customers who alerted us and provided us with information.

I was scanning Blue Bell's website to find out if its new Salted Caramel Cookie flavor was out yet and was actually unaware of the incident until the statement above suddenly took over my screen. If, like me, you didn't know anything about the incident, you wouldn't have much of a clue as to what this statement was all about. Blue Bell pushed a bad-news break onto me when it should be pushing this kind of thing to a digital newsroom.

IN-HOUSE VIDEO INTERVIEW

In-house video interviews feel more authentic than statements, but they are highly controlled. These are especially appealing when the subject matter is challenging. I have several former television reporters on my team who, when a crisis hits a client, create an interview set at a client's location and conduct a video recorded interview with the client just as they did when they worked in a newsroom.

With a camera rolling, they put the client through the paces of a challenging interview. They ask the same tough questions an active reporter would ask, and if the client's responses aren't favorable for the brand, they do a take two, a take three, or as many retakes as necessary. After the interview, our team edits the footage into a cohesive B-roll package, the client approves the final product, and we distribute it to news outlets. Will the media use it? Given the massive reductions in newsroom staffing over the past few decades, it's increasingly likely, but honestly, we don't really care. We have provided the media an on-camera interview, and they're not going to get any other information.

Here is an example of how a company effectively created an in-house interview.

In January 2024, shortly after takeoff, Alaska Airlines flight 1282 had to make an emergency landing after a door plug on the aircraft detached midair. The plane, a Boeing 737 MAX 9, was later found to be missing the bolts that were supposed to fasten the door plug into place. Although there were no fatalities, passengers were certainly traumatized, and the news media was in a frenzy.[310]

This was not the first time that Boeing 737s had been put into the spotlight for aircraft malfunctions. In 2018, a Boeing 737 crashed, killing 189 passengers, and in 2019, another 737 crashed, killing 157 passengers—a total of 346 deaths in five months. Both crashes were found to be linked to problems with a flight stabilizing feature on the Boeing 737.[311]

Boeing responded to the first crash by blaming the pilot and issuing the airline a "flight crew operational manual." The company said the plane was safe and it was an isolated incident. Following the second crash, Boeing once again defended the aircraft's safety, issuing a public statement expressing empathy without accepting fault. As a result, Boeing received widespread criticism for their delayed response and lack of responsibility.[312] This crisis led to several investigations, and in 2021, Boeing agreed to pay a settlement of $2.5 billion in charges.[313] In addition, the Federal Aviation Administration grounded all Boeing 737 MAX 9s with similar door plugs, leading to canceled flights and a net loss of $11.8 billion to Boeing's annual revenue.[314]

The method part of all of this came into view when CEO Dave Calhoun responded by recording an in-house interview. He told his employees:

When I got that picture [of the missing door plug], all I could think about—I didn't know what happened so whoever was supposed to be in the seat next to that hole in the airplane…I've got kids, I've got grandkids and so do you. This stuff matters. Every detail matters. We're going to approach this, number one, acknowledging our mistake. We're going to approach it with 100 percent and complete transparency every step of the way.…We are going to work with the NTSB who is investigating the accident itself to find out what the cause is.[315]

Clips of Calhoun's interview were then distributed to news outlets across the internet.

What made this method effective? First, Calhoun's emotions were on display.[316] He showed emotional distress about the incident, and because he was addressing employees directly, it was apparent the entire company was affected by the gravity of the situation.

The combination of Boeing's immediate response and method of delivery settled better with stakeholders compared to delayed and high-control responses in 2018 and 2019.[317]

BACKGROUND BRIEFING

Typically, an interview on background is conducted to provide insights to a reporter anonymously. It allows you to share information but not be quoted. The standard rules for reporters, found in the Associated Press Stylebook, are:

1. Whenever possible, pursue information on the record.
2. When a source insists on background or off-the-record ground rules, do so if the material is information and not opinion or speculation, and is vital to the news report; if the information is not available on the record; and finally, if the source is reliable.[318]

Background briefings are high-control, low-authenticity tools because the phrase "sources said..." in an article is perceived as less credible than an attributed quote. While there is some risk a reporter will break the rules and quote a source who preferred to remain anonymous, it's rare. Add an extra layer of protection by informing the reporter you are recording the background briefing before it begins. Then be sure to state the rules of engagement up front for the recording.

I have successfully arranged for clients to give background briefings and found them useful, not only because they convey information and allow anonymity, but also because they settle a spokesperson down. If a client can talk to a reporter on background just once and deliver good messaging, they will fear interacting with reporters much less and, therefore, tend to be more willing to go on the record when the time is right.

INTERVIEW OF RECORD

Conducted by telephone, an interview of record has one objective: to establish narrative control. You can make going on the record a high-control, high-authenticity maneuver by following this procedure:

1. Schedule a phone interview with one select reporter from one media outlet reputable enough to amplify the brand's message to its stakeholder population.
2. Secure a quiet conference room with a speakerphone and a long wall.
3. Using flip-chart paper and markers, create posters with the key messages your spokesperson needs to convey to the reporter regarding the incident. Dedicate one poster to your spokesperson's "headline quote"—the most important message to convey in the interview.
4. Write additional anticipated questions and prepared responses on other flip-chart pages. Use the Predictive Interviewing Model to ensure all six question types are included. Be sure to pose difficult or uncomfortable questions. If your spokesperson says, "I don't like that question..." or "I'm not going to answer that question," don't let them have their way. Use the PIM to persuade them the reporter will ask difficult questions, and they need to respond.
5. Affix each poster to the long wall of the conference room.
6. Practice the interview with your spokesperson. Provide bridges and flags (see the Messenger chapter for explanation) to help them pivot gracefully toward positive messages. If the situation

is complex, it may be helpful to have a second spokesperson participate in the interview. The two can respond to each other's points and even interrupt a line of questioning by asking each other softball questions while the reporter is listening.

7. To start the interview, introduce the spokesperson and the reporter, set a time limit, and then serve as a "Vanna White"–type presenter as the interview proceeds, silently walking the poster wall and pointing to the best responses to the questions asked.

8. Conclude the call at the set time and follow up afterward with any details needed by the reporter. It's a good practice to record the interview for reference in case the reporter mischaracterizes a response and a correction is warranted.

END-AROUND INTERVIEW

In discussing the knowability of things, Daniel Kahneman wrote, "We believe we understand the past, which implies that the future also should be knowable, but in fact we understand the past less than we believe we do."[319] What happens, though, if a reporter thinks they already know everything about what your brand has done wrong and shows no signs of being objective?

This happened to a start-up food company called Sea to Table. In 2018, three reporters published an Associated Press story entitled, "AP Investigation: Fish billed as local isn't always local."[320] The three-thousand-plus-word story was an investigation into the traceability of fresh-caught fish, an issue that has plagued the seafood industry. Sea to Table claimed to have established a method for significantly improving traceability and had built a long list of clients who were impressed by the company's work to bring authenticity to the sustainable seafood movement.

The AP investigation was incredibly thorough. To gather evidence that the company wasn't delivering on its own traceability standards and code of conduct, the reporters enlisted DNA scientists, used hidden cameras at fish markets, and interviewed a number of Sea to Table customers who were shocked and dismayed by the evidence. It's fair to say the reporters were fully invested in their story, having spent months piecing together an account that fit a sinister narrative. No matter what Sea to Table CEO Sean Dimin might have said in response to questions, the AP's through-line was set. Proof of that is in the interview-to-publish cycle time. Dimin granted an interview to the AP and spent considerable time—more than two hours by his account—explaining how their evidence might be interpreted differently, yet the story published minutes after the interview.

How is it possible to write an objective article of this size, to include Sea to Table's perspective, so fast? This tells me the article was already written. A few quotes from Dimin were simply sprinkled in to create an illusion of objectivity.

An end-around interview might have helped Sea to Table had it understood what was happening. If a narrative is already set, you'll know because a reporter will call and basically say, "We're going to print/on air with a story about your brand in a few minutes and just want to get your reaction." In such a case, providing more information to the reporter only helps them validate a narrative they have already created, which means there's greater risk of saying something else damaging versus turning the narrative around. The solution? Get an end-around interview. Find a different reporter at a competing media outlet. Move quickly to tell your story—bad news and all—under more of your control, using your key messages. The aim of an end-around interview is to set up a counter-narrative that diminishes the ill effects of the story about to be told by another media outlet. Will the original reporter and news outlet be furious with you? Probably, but why do you care? They're out to torpedo your brand! Worry less about damaging a relationship with a reporter than defending your brand.

SERIAL SESSIONS

Certain crisis situations push multiple reporters—both print and broadcast—into a full-court press against a brand. Before relenting to the bad decision of submitting to the feeding frenzy of a press conference, consider scheduling a series of interviews in a condensed amount of time, one right after the other. Find a fairly large, but quiet, space in which a single camera and reporter can fit with you and your trained spokesperson. Walk the news crew in one door, have them set up, interview your client for not more than ten minutes, then have them pack up and walk out a different door to exit. Take a quick break, get your client refreshed on a key message, take a few deep breaths, and repeat until all the news stations have an interview.

As manufactured as this feels, my experience has proven that reporters don't really mind this setup. They get their interview, they get their sound bites, and they get out of there for their next assignments that day. The advantage for the client is by the second interview, the agreed-upon key messages pop out like cash from an ATM.

THIRD-PARTY INTERVIEW

Third-party advocates for your brand who are viewed as objective can be useful messengers in a bad-news break. They may include many types of subject matter experts or—like preachers, politicians, or professors—may be character witnesses. Cultivating these relationships takes time and energy, but doing so can pay dividends when trouble comes. The trick in using third parties is to understand their relative value.

Technical experts can be pulled into service when the nature of an issue or incident is not widely known. Scientists, engineers, chemists, and accountants are great advocates when problems can be fixed by simply being more knowledgeable of the issue or field than the audience you need to reach. No matter how sophisticated stakeholders may be, they are highly persuaded by experts because people tend to believe in the "myth of a technological fix, a myth that assures us that it is always possible to develop a complex technocratic solution to problems caused by human frailty."[321]

Using technical experts works well when competency is questioned. When character is in the crosshairs, it's a good idea to call on clergy, philosophers, psychologists, politicians, etc., to testify as character witnesses for your brand. The angle of messaging delivered by character messengers should focus on intent and track record. In Benoit's Image Repair Typology, this is known as "bolstering."

Both tactics work because humans, by nature, believe authority figures. Persuasion expert Robert Cialdini explains, "Conforming to the dictates of authority figures has always had genuine practical advantages for us. Early on, these people (for example, parents, teachers) knew more than we did, and taking their advice proved beneficial."[322]

SOCIAL ENGAGEMENT

Actively engaging stakeholders via social media during a crisis, using the brand's official channels and handles, is fraught with risk. This is due to the exposure it creates in the land of anonymous trolls and malicious content. In fact, social media may be the very venue amplifying an issue and making it a crisis. In its most recent survey of 2,600 risk managers from thirty-three industries, the global insurance company Aon reported: "damage to brand and reputation" is second only to "economic slowdown..." on its list of concerns.[323] The report reads, "Widespread use of social media puts brands at risk for long-term negative consequences, both in public perception and in the marketplace." That said, social media cannot be ignored.

Social engagement requires trading control for authenticity, which can make an already-nervous chief decision-maker or spokesperson even jumpier. A threshold guide can help. It sets the rules of engagement for the brand, so it doesn't overreact to posts or underreact to reputation-damaging trends. At the Level 1 threshold, track and monitor the volume of angry commentary and frustration venting. Most social media listening platforms can discern a narrative pattern from the comments posted. The Level 2 threshold is crossed when misinformation or patently false statements begin to appear. These may warrant well-worded corrections, but take care not to inflame stakeholders. At Level 3, negative commentary begins to snowball and trend. At this point, social media sentiment becomes the news, and you cannot avoid active engagement. Use written-statement messaging to assert narrative control and be prepared to stay in it for the duration. Once engagement begins, it has to continue until the issue runs out of steam.

PRESS CONFERENCE

What are the odds that putting a spokesperson under hot lights in front of a group of frothing reporters, with cameras rolling, is going to turn out well? Press conferences feel very authentic to viewers because, in their traditional format, a subject-matter expert (SME) spokesperson is quite literally exposed to a barrage of questions, sometimes on a wide-range of subjects.

On a positive note, the willingness to put your messenger in that position demonstrates courage and may be rewarded with positive commentary if the impressions, quotes, and responses meet or exceed stakeholder expectations. Press conferences are low-control environments, but you can offset that lack of control by setting up the venue using the tool below for guidance.

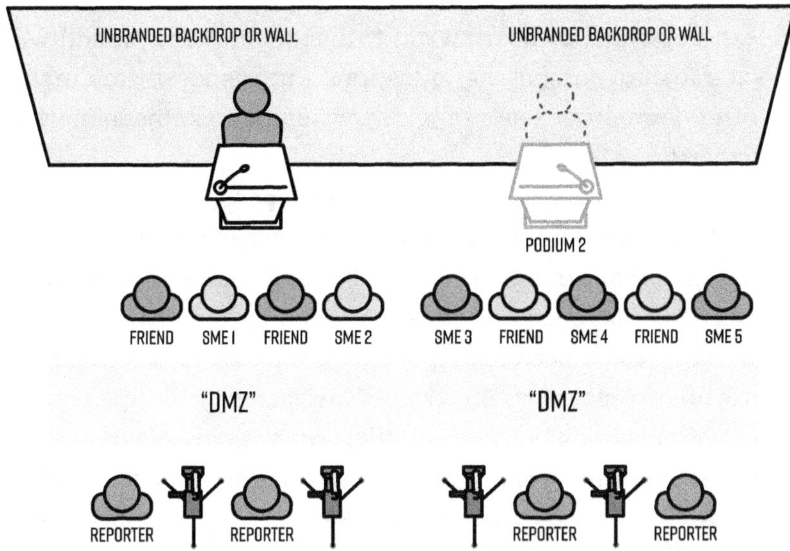

Like the holding statement jig discussed previously, this template can be helpful to rapid response teams who may feel they have no choice but to hold a press conference. A few features worth pointing out:

1. Two podiums. The senior communication leader occupies one podium; the subject-matter expert, chief decision-maker, or another appointed spokesperson occupies the other. The senior communication leader acts as the facilitator during the press conference, setting the ground rules, timing, and agenda. The senior communication leader may also field all questions first, reword them if necessary, and serve them up to the spokesperson at the second podium.

2. Backdrop and front row. Be mindful of the backdrop behind the podiums, especially when bad news is breaking. Make it as bland and uninteresting as possible—no logos, no step-and-repeat signage, and no people. Having people stand behind speakers in fig-leaf poses produces an awkward effect. Instead, put these people in the front-row seats. Call up subject-matter

experts seated in the front row to make statements, or address character or competency questions. Put friends or staff in the other front-row seats to whisper advice to subject-matter experts.

3. The "demilitarized zone" (DMZ) and space. One tough question answered with one poor response can prompt a chain reaction that can unnerve even the most seasoned spokesperson. Packing reporters close together accelerates this energy. Creating space between reporters can reduce the likelihood of a feeding frenzy erupting, typically triggered by the first gotcha question. Gotchas feel more like stunts than objective journalism, but they aren't just possible, they are probable once a press conference gets underway. As CenterPoint Energy CEO Jason Wells learned, proceed with caution.

In July 2024, Hurricane Beryl struck the Houston region. The storm pushed 2.6 million electric customers into the dark, with CenterPoint Energy responsible for about 2.2 million of those failures. Outages persisted for twelve days, contributing to twenty-three deaths and causing roughly $1.2 billion in damages to the company's infrastructure.[324]

CenterPoint faced widespread criticism in the aftermath of the storm due to the CEO's controversial press conference during the crisis. Wells appeared before a room full of reporters and photojournalists to discuss the company's efforts to restore power. In that setting, he was filmed and photographed sitting on a couch in the CenterPoint headquarters office. On the wall was a company logo and a thermostat reading a comfortable 70 degrees.[325]

The interview backdrop, not the interview itself, sparked outrage. The thermostat symbolized a disconnect between the utility company and its customers, especially since it had urged customers to keep their thermostats at less-than-comfortable temperatures while repairs were underway.[326]

ONE ADDITIONAL TOOL: THE BLUE-RIBBON PANEL

What if the subject-matter experts you put in front of the press at a press conference don't seem to have the credibility needed to address a complex situation? As suggested earlier in the Messenger chapter of the book, specially commissioned groups, also known as blue-ribbon panels, can be effective devices.

Blue-ribbon panels get assembled to perform in-depth, root-cause analyses about why and how an issue or incident occurred. Typically, panels comprise respected outside experts from a variety of disciplines who operate with a significant autonomy. Commissions and panels, while having low control, offer a high level of authenticity that other methods cannot.

In the wake of multiple cyclospora outbreaks across the US, Fresh Express, the salad and leafy green producer, set up a twelve-member blue-ribbon panel "comprised of scientists with deep expertise in the biology of the cyclospora cayetanensis organism, food safety, outbreak response, and public health. The independent panel, chaired by noted infectious disease and food safety expert, Dr. Michael T. Osterholm, was charged with studying the little-understood cyclospora parasite and identifying controls to limit further outbreaks." The panel produced a report with thirty recommendations for the prevention and response to contamination incidents.[327]

The value a blue-ribbon panel provides is time. Because they are deliberative, they can take much more time than what is offered inside the Tick-Tock Box. All questions from stakeholders or even the media can be deferred. Then when the time is right, a report can be issued, and a press conference held with the panel experts and the brand.

Blue-ribbon panels are great tools when time is needed to sort through complex situations, but a few downsides come along for the ride. First, panels are only credible if they are objective. The information the panel decides to report cannot be ethically quashed or skewed, so a brand must be prepared to fully accept and respond to the panel's findings. Second, a blue-ribbon panel's work doesn't end a crisis; it extends a crisis. When findings are released, bad news gets fresh legs.

It's smart to view the options in the 2x2 as discrete, but not exclusive to one another. It's not uncommon for an incident to lend itself to the use of multiple options in parallel or in sequence, which is signified in the Rapid Response Model diagram by the little yin-yang arrow circle labeled "Release." Just as a well-coordinated military might combine air, sea, and land forces to confront a security threat, rapid response teams can combine tactics to reach stakeholders quickly and establish narrative control.

CHAPTER 12

THE EARNED REPUTATION FLYWHEEL

"It takes twenty years to build a reputation and five minutes to ruin it."

—Warren Buffett

For almost twenty years, Six Flags Great Adventure in New Jersey held the record for having the tallest and fastest roller coaster in the world—the Kingda Ka. Built in 2005 by a Swiss company known for pushing the limits of engineering, the ride stood 457 feet tall and launched riders to 128 miles per hour in a matter of seconds. It's been described as falling out of a forty-five-story skyscraper while moving at the speed of a Formula One race car. The ride lasts only half a minute, but the thrill is unmatched—so much so, that people travel globally to ride it.[328]

What made (the ride was taken down in 2025) Kingda Ka a remarkable feat of engineering wasn't just the speed or height; it was that there was no onboard power source. Nothing drove it forward but gravity, design, and momentum.

How do roller coasters run without an engine? Physics.

Roller coasters function through a conversion process that transfers energy between kinetic and potential forms. At the start, a launch mechanism propels the train up the track, building potential energy the higher it climbs. The higher it goes, the more energy it stores. Once a train of cars reaches a peak, gravity takes over, pulling it downward and turning that stored energy into speed, otherwise known as kinetic energy. This transfer of energy is what drives the ride forward again and again.[329]

Why start this chapter with a physics lesson?

In crisis, speed and momentum are valuable. While a crisis can feel like a freefall, if you've built the right systems, that same fall can power a comeback. The trick is learning how to harness the energy. Just like a coaster doesn't stop at the bottom, neither should a brand in crisis. The drop can be the beginning of a recovery for your brand's reputation.

Neil Culbertson and Laurel Kennedy said this about the phase of reputation management: "The most overlooked aspect of crisis communication is the recovery phase. As the crisis wanes and operations normalize, it's easy to think things will just go back to normal. Think again. There is now a 'new normal.'"[330]

It makes sense. You can't pretend a crisis didn't happen. Something triggered bad news requiring you to work your way through a crisis, and that something was a break with stakeholder expectations. You're not the same as you were before; you've gone through a defining moment and have to find a new normal to remain compatible with your stakeholders' new expectations.

The road to recovery is not a one-size-fits-all approach. Incidents that strike at people's deepest values or fears naturally make stakeholders more wary of a brand, and many will demand credible proof of change before they are willing to trust again. Difficult, however, does not mean impossible. With a clear demonstration of character and competence, a brand can regain its footing.

Trust must be earned back over time. It won't be regained overnight or with one press release. At this stage, your actions speak far louder than words. You need to consistently deliver on promises and prove that a past breakdown was an exception, not a rule.

Because it's such a stark case, let's go back to Astronomer. You'll recall that CEO Andy Byron and Chief People Officer Kristin Cabot were caught in what appeared to be an intimate moment on a stadium kiss cam during a Coldplay concert. Within hours, the video went viral, and the internet quickly discovered that both executives were married—to other people. Suddenly, two of the company's top leaders were caught in the center of the headlines. Both were placed on administrative leave pending an internal investigation, and within days, Byron resigned.

In the court of public opinion, the reputations they had built over a lifetime were toast in a matter of hours. If you were advising the pair, what would you recommend they do next to recover their reputations? How do start to earn trust back? Now turn the question to others who have found themselves in the news: Sean "Diddy" Combs, Elon Musk, Ellen DeGeneres, Amber Heard, and Kanye West.[331]

At its core, restoration means facing a hard truth: Reputation isn't given back; it must be re-earned. You have to prove to your stakeholders, through your actions, that you deserve to be trusted again. Charlie Munger says it like this:

By and large the people who have this ethos win in life, and they don't win just money, not just honors. They win the respect, the deserved trust of the people they deal with, and there is huge pleasure in life to be obtained from getting deserved trust.[332]

The starting point for restoration is to genuinely deserve the trust you seek to rebuild. When a brand, institutional or personal, behaves in a way you would trust if you were the customer on the other side, it's on the right track. Once you earn back trust, you can begin generating momentum.

Earning and building reputation first means, however, that your brand is interesting.

What makes something interesting? In 1971, a Northern Illinois University professor named Murray S. Davis wrote a paper entitled, "That's Interesting!" A few insights from it:

- "A new theory will be noticed only when it denies an old truth."
- "An interesting proposition [is] always the negation of an accepted one."
- "All interesting propositions...involve...radical distinction."[333]

If you study Professor Davis's insights, you recognize their simple genius. "Interesting" helps a brand talk about itself in the affirmative. It is differentiating. Negating an accepted proposition helps a brand avoid saying things that are obvious, irrelevant, or absurd—a triple threat to being interesting.

On the same subject, the legendary ad man Bill Bernbach said, "If you stand for something, you will always find some people for you and some against you. If you stand for nothing, you will find nobody against you, and nobody for you."[334] "Interesting," as it turns out, means not everyone is going to love you.

Building reputation requires standing for something different. Contrast your brand to what is believed to be true and synthesize the contrast down to a single line a competitor can't easily replicate. Break a habit. Flaunt your flaws. Challenge an assumption. Zig when the world zags.

Sacrifice is also a characteristic of what it takes to be interesting. Another Bernbach quote makes the point. After his agency decided to exit the very profitable cigarette advertising business, he told an *LA Times* reporter, "I don't feel a principle is a principle until it costs you money."[335] The same is true for reputation restoration. You'll know you're on the road to normal when you're spending money to invest in reputation. Rebuilding reputation requires earning attention, and earning attention costs money.

Not only do you have to be interesting and invest money to earn people's attention, building reputation today means facing the obnoxious realities mentioned earlier:

- Algorithm-based robot reporters are increasingly responsible for creating the content of newsfeeds.
- Relationships with reporters matter more than ever because fewer of them exist.

Navigating your way out of a bad-news break can feel like climbing a mountain. Each step feels precarious and requires more energy than the previous one. The view from "Mount New Normal" is pretty good, though, so it's worth the climb. Brands that have created a reservoir of goodwill and a social license to operate—the building blocks of a good reputation—don't have as far to climb, but both require purposeful energy.

Jim Collins authored several books—*Good to Great, How the Mighty Fall,* and the very cool monograph, *Turning the Flywheel.* Collins provided the method I'm still trying to perfect—the work in progress is shown below. This "Earned Reputation Flywheel" attempts to illustrate how a brand might go about generating purposeful positive energy to find its new normal.

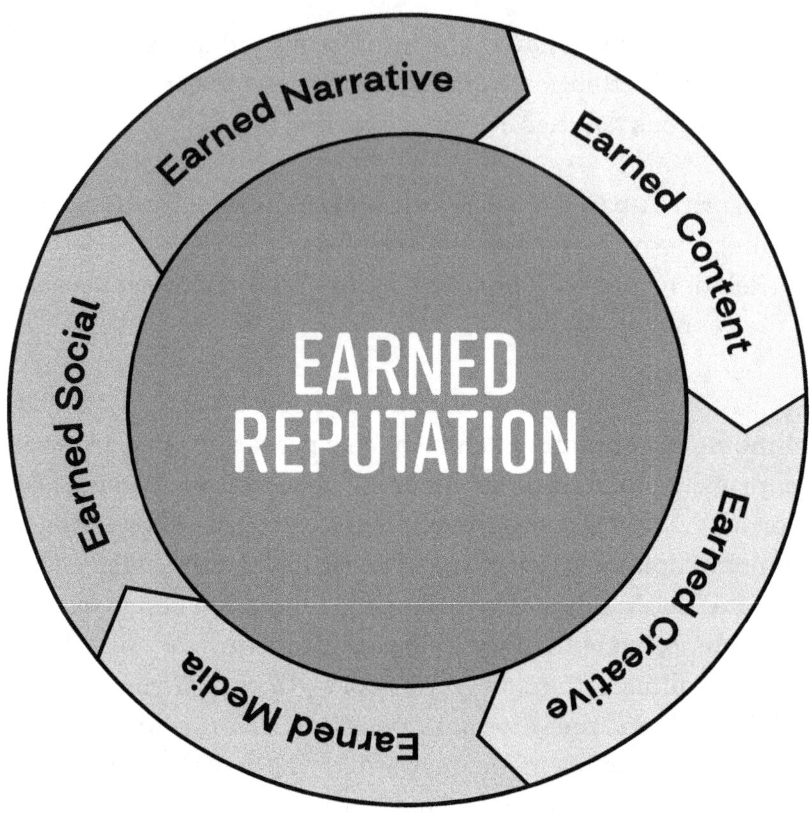

1. Earned Narrative. Earned narrative is the interesting story you want to tell your stakeholders. Professor Murray Davis told us to be interesting to create distinction and start the flywheel turning. This is the place to find your differentiation and shape it, like Kurt Vonnegut may have done, into a narrative for your brand.

2. Earned Content. Earned content is aligned with your narrative platform. Produce it by generating blog posts, Substack articles, podcasts, speaking opportunities, and earned media coverage. Put it all in a digital newsroom hub on your website to showcase your brand.

3. Earned Creative. Earned creative—brand identity, video, design, infographics, and animation—forms the packaging

around your earned content to make it attention grabbing. Remember, you have about 8.95 seconds to make me care.

4. Earned Media. Earned media attracts the attention of influencers and the press, including robot reporters whose voracious appetites can't resist trending ideas. They amplify the content in successive posts and articles read by an ever-mushrooming number of outlets, growing your brand equity and reinforcing your narrative. It's a cycle that creates momentum.

5. Earned Social. Earned social shares the content package with your core, organically grown audience through social channels like LinkedIn, Facebook, Instagram, and TikTok. Use paid promotion for social posts to add more energy to the flywheel.

The flywheel works because it's earned. Earned is more credible and authentic to audiences than ads; it generates more interest/word-of-mouth than other mediums, because it can keep pace with the market's speed; it has unmatched amplification capability due to news syndication and sharing by social influencers; it has a more durable effect on people's recall ability because it is interactive; and its value can be measured more easily than ever before.

The Earned Reputation Flywheel shifts the polarity of brand outreach work from push to pull. If you're trying to push a story to stakeholders without an Earned Reputation Flywheel, you're missing the opportunity to pull an audience toward you. You're substituting the quick hit of a paid ad for the harder but far more rewarding and reputation-building work of creating an interesting narrative worthy of attention and affection.

In any industry, things go wrong. Products can fail, safety standards can be missed, data can get leaked, and sometimes employees do things that spark headlines. When you have the Earned Reputation Flywheel in motion, you can harness its energy to quickly earn back trust by popping the Rapid Response Model's parachute, skillfully navigating a crisis, and climbing back up to your normal and expected trajectory.

SPEAK THE FUTURE INTO BEING

Belief-driven buyers now make up a majority of American consumers. What do they believe? Generally, it's this:

> The government is dysfunctional, so you can't trust it. All the news is fake, so you can't trust it. Who can I trust? I'm going to trust brands that take a stand on issues important to me.[336]

When a brand publicly supports a consumer's position on a significant issue, versus staying silent, most belief-driven buyers will buy the brand exclusively, more often, and they will pay a premium price for it. They'll also become advocates for the brand, actively defending it in a crisis.

Brands that work to make the world a better place are going to win. Brands that simply force their messaging onto people's radar through the brute force of paid ads will eventually lose the right to be at consumers' tables.

Brands willing to earn interest can build a core following of evangelical consumers who trust their products. They'll follow the roadmap Douglas Atkin laid out in his book *The Culting of Brands*. Atkin writes that creating community and rolling with the punches of the relationship are keys to brand affinity. Like package design, owned and paid marketing will always have a role, but the Earned Reputation Flywheel is winning in today's attention economy because consumers interacting with content get to pull a brand closer.[337]

This is the world we live in. It's been called reputation management, public relations, marketing, and marketing communications. None of them really fit. It's not advertising, nor is it purely content marketing. It is the carefully constructed fusion of all those capabilities necessary to support a brand.

In today's earned-interest, attention economy, successful brands will literally speak the future into being by embracing a manifesto of sorts:

- We will build an interesting brand narrative that pulls attention toward what we offer. In doing so, we will be worthy of people's most perishable asset—their attention.
- We will empower others to share our product and brand message through creatively packaged content capable of making news.
- We will never censor voices opposed to what we create; instead, we will embrace the fact that our offering is not for everyone.
- If something goes wrong, we will move quickly to protect our brand on behalf of those who believe in what we do. They will advocate for us, because we have invested in building a reservoir of goodwill.

Speaking the future into being requires harnessing all the power of the Earned Reputation Flywheel. Doing that well requires special attention and commitment, but isn't that the case with anything and everything we seek to do well?

This book is about bad news, but intertwined in every idea and model I have presented is the uplifting reality that brands can successfully ride out even the roughest storms. That's the good news I want to leave you with: People still need what your brand offers, and they're willing to trust again, if trust is earned. Using the tools provided in this book, you can support any brand sincerely interested in serving them, even in the toughest times. Remember, the end of a crisis is not the end of the story. In fact, it's the beginning of a new journey.

JUST A LITTLE MORE BREAKING BAD NEWS

As a thank you for picking up a copy of *Breaking Bad News* and a reward for making it all the way to this page, I would be very happy to send you a signed bookplate at no charge. Email your name and postal mailing information to BBN2@hahn.agency, and I'll respond if I am not inside some Tick-Tock Box.

If you are interested in spokesperson training, please visit the hahn.agency website. You are also welcome to visit the website to download presentation-ready colorized versions of some models shown in this book.

I appreciate your interest and wish you many sleep-filled nights.

ACKNOWLEDGMENTS

Defining moments mark the life of someone who has built a career frequently punctuated by crisis events, and I thank several amazing mentors for allowing me to see firsthand how they navigated exceptionally difficult and high-stakes issues. Kerry Tate, Rusty Brashear, David Doolittle, Nan McRaven, Asanga Weerakoon, and Dan Harrison very deservedly stand out. Tucker Perkins has to be mentioned as well with gratitude for his trust in me as we tapped our way through complexity. Finally, this book would not have been possible without the inspiration provided by David Pulatie, a model-making genius and big-picture thinker.

All of these very special people appreciate the grit and resilience needed for truly managing crises, as did my mother, Arlene. In the minutes after a tornado utterly and completely destroyed our northeast Iowa farm at 5:44 p.m. on Sunday, November 9, 1975, Mom—as we stood where barns and buildings had just minutes earlier—said to our family, "Listen, we're alive, and we're going to get through this."

Now, that's a crisis manager talking.

Many thanks to my colleagues at Hahn Marketing & PR for

their support and encouragement to bring this 2nd Edition of the book to life, and a special acknowledgment to Kalei Aurit for her smart research and true curiosity for the subject.

For Laurie, who makes all things possible, and to Harper and Haleigh for seeing me through the crisis of a lifetime.

CITATIONS

INTRODUCTION

1   Rahm Emanuel, "Rahm Emanuel on the Opportunities of Crisis," interview by *The Wall Street Journal*, November 19, 2008, https://www.youtube.com/watch?v=_mzcbXi1Tkk.

2   Saul D. Alinsky, *Rules for Radicals: A Practical Primer for Realistic Radicals* (Vintage, 1989).

3   John F. Kennedy, "Remarks at the Convocation of the United Negro College Fund," Indianapolis, Indiana, April 12, 1959, transcript, https://www.jfklibrary.org/archives/other-resources/john-f-kennedy-speeches/indianapolis-in-19590412.

4   Victor H. Mair, "Danger + Opportunity ≠ Crisis: How a Misunderstanding about Chinese Characters Has Led Many Astray," Pinyin, revised September 2009, accessed August 16, 2019, http://www.pinyin.info/chinese/crisis.html.

5   "Leadership Lessons for Uncertain Times: A Discussion with Eric Rosenbach," Harvard Online, November 7, 2024, https://www.harvardonline.harvard.edu/leadership-lessons-uncertain-times-discussion-eric-rosenbach.

6   James Charlton, *The Military Quotations Book* (St. Martin's Press, 2002), 85.

CHAPTER 1

7   Andrew Caesar-Gordon, "Lessons to Learn from a Product Recall." PRWeek, October 28, 2015, accessed August 16, 2019, https://www.prweek.com/article/1357209/lessons-learn-product-recall.

8   Catherine Boal, "Cadbury Contamination Proves Costly," Confectionary News, August 1, 2006, https://www.confectionerynews.com/Article/2006/08/02/Cadbury-contamination-proves-costly/.

9   Vanessa Golembewski, "Bad News for Fireball Drinkers?" Refinery29, October 28, 2014, accessed August 16, 2019, https://www.refinery29.com/en-us/2014/10/76987/fireball-recall-antifreeze.

10 Scott Galloway, "In a Crisis, You Must Overreact," Medium, March 22, 2020, https://marker.medium.com/in-a-crisis-you-must-overreact-955074781ead.

11 John Kelly, "Why Does News 'Break'?," Mashed Radish, May 23, 2017, https://mashedradish.com/2017/05/23/why-does-news-break.

12 Benjamin Snyder, "7 Insights from Legendary Investor Warren Buffett," CNBC, May 1, 2017, accessed August 16, 2019, https://www.cnbc.com/2017/05/01/7-insights-from-legendary-investor-warren-buffett.html.

13 Daniel Epstein, "Excerpt: 'The Lincolns,'" from *The Lincolns: Portrait of a Marriage* (Ballantine, 2008), NPR, July 30, 2008, https://www.npr.org/templates/story/story.php?storyId=93255875.

14 Bill Coletti, *Critical Moments: The New Mindset of Reputation Management* (Lioncrest Publishing, 2017), 42.

15 Leon Bracey, November 6, 2013, "The Importance of Business Reputation," *Business in Focus*, https://leonthewriter.wordpress.com/wp-content/uploads/2015/05/business-reputation-pdf.pdf.

16 Larissa Faw, "Report: Majority of Global Consumers Are 'Belief-Driven Buyers,'" October 2, 2018, MediaPost, October 2, 2018, https://www.mediapost.com/publications/article/325911/report-majority-of-global-consumers-are-belief-d.html?edition=111178.

17 Steven Fink, *Crisis Communications: The Definitive Guide to Managing the Message* (McGraw-Hill Education, 2013), 249–251, 46.

18 W. Timothy Coombs, *Ongoing Crisis Communication: Planning, Managing, and Responding (NULL)* 4th ed., (Sage Publications, Inc, 2014), 8.

19 Robert C. Chandler, "The Role of First Language Reversion in Communication and Outreach: An Integrative, Multilingual Approach," presentation, 5th International Disaster and Risk Conference, August 2014, accessed January 17, 2016, https://www.slideshare.net/GRFDavos/chandlerthe-role-of-first-language-reversion-in-communication-and-outreach.

20 United States Coast Guard Auxiliary, Surface Operations Risk Calculation Worksheet, U.S. Department of Homeland Security, 2009, accessed January 17, 2019, http://rdept.cgaux.org/documents/GAR%20 Model%20 Surface%20Ops.pdf.

21 Tali Sharot, "The Optimism Bias," *Current Biology* 21, no. 23 (December 6, 2011): R941–R945, https://doi.org/10.1016/j.cub.2011.10.030.

22 "Boston Marathon Bombing," Federal Bureau of Investigation, accessed July 28, 2025, https://www.fbi.gov/history/famous-cases/boston-marathon-bombing.

23 Nassim Nicholas Taleb, *Antifragile: Things that Gain from Disorder* (Random House, 2012).

24 Kevin Granville, "Complexifier, Mr. Bezos? It is a Real Word, Not Just in English," *New York Times*, February 8, 2019, https://www.nytimes.com/2019/02/08/business/complexifier-meaning-definition.html?module=inline.

25 Robert Buckman, *How to Break Bad News: A Guide for Health Care Professionals* (Johns Hopkins University Press, 1992).

26 Josh Tapper, "Dr. Robert Buckman, Renowned Oncologist, Comedian and Star Columnist, Dead at 63," *The Star*, October 10, 2011, https://www.thestar.com/news/gta/2011/10/10/dr_robert_buckman_renowned_oncologist_comedian_and_star_columnist_dead_at_63.html.

27 Robert Buckman, "Breaking Bad News," *99% Invisible* (podcast), episode 306, May 8, 2018, 9:10 and 25:08, https://99percentinvisible.org/episode/breaking-bad-news.

28 Walter F. Baile et al., "SPIKES—A Six-Step Protocol for Delivering Bad News: Application to the Patient with Cancer," *The Oncologist* 5, no. 4 (2000): 302–311, https://doi.org/10.1634/theoncologist.5-4-302.

CHAPTER 2

29 Alfred Korzybski, "A Non-Aristotelian System and Its Necessity for Rigour in Mathematics and Physics," in *Science and Sanity: An Introduction to Non-Aristotelian Systems and General Semantics* (International Non-Aristotelian Library Publishing Company, 1933).

30 Tren Griffin, *Charlie Munger: The Complete Investor* (Columbia Business School Publishing, 2015).

31 Charlie Munger, "A Lesson Elementary Worldly Wisdom as it Relates to Investment Management & Business," speech delivered at University of Southern California, Marshall School of Business, 1994, transcript, accessed October 8, 2025, https://fs.blog/great-talks/a-lesson-on-worldly-wisdom/.

32 Munger, "A Lesson Elementary Worldly Wisdom."

33 Charles T. Munger, *Poor Charlie's Almanack: The Wit and Wisdom of Charles T. Munger*, 3rd ed. (Walsworth Publishing Company, 2005), 56.

34 Peter Bevelin, *Seeking Wisdom: From Darwin to Munger*, 3rd ed. (PCA Publication, 2007), 27.

35 Mikael Krogerus and Roman Tschäppeler, *The Decision Book: Fifty Models for Strategic Thinking*, 2nd ed. (W.W. Norton & Company, 2011), 6.

36 Munger, *Poor Charlie's Almanack*, 166.

37 Nassim Taleb, *The Black Swan: The Impact of the Highly Improbable* (Random House, 2007), xxi-xxii.

38 David Rosenberg, *The Hidden Holmes: His Theory of Torts in History* (Harvard University Press, 1996), 233.

39 Eric Dezenhall, *Glass Jaw: A Manifesto for Defending Fragile Reputations in an Age of Instant Scandal* (Twelve/Hachette Book Group, 2014), 80.

40 Bevelin, *Seeking Wisdom*, 190.

41 Joseph Voros, "The Futures Cone, Use and History," The Voroscope, February 2, 2017, https://thevoroscope.com/2017/02/24/the-futures-cone-use-and-history/.

42 Leon Festinger, *A Theory of Cognitive Dissonance* (Stanford University Press, 1957).

43 Gary Cronkhite, "Autonomic Correlates of Dissonance and Attitude Change." *Speech Monographs* 33, no. 4 (November 1966): 392–399, https://doi.org/10.1080/03637756609375506.

44 E. Tory Higgins et al., "Dissonance Motivation: Its Nature, Persistence, and Reinstatement," *Journal of Experimental Social Psychology* 15, no. 1 (January 1979): 16–34, https://doi.org/10.1016/0022-1031(79)90015-5.

45 M.P Zanna and J. Cooper, "Dissonance and the Pill: An Attribution Approach to Studying the Arousal Properties of Dissonance," *Journal of Personality and Social Psychology* 29, no. 5 (1974): 703–709, https://psycnet.apa.org/doiLanding?doi=10.1037%2Fh0036651.

46 Krogerus and Tschäppeler, *The Decision Book*, 50.

47 Robert B. Cialdini, *Influence: The Psychology of Persuasion*, rev. ed. (Harper Business, 2006), 59, 60–82.

48 Ralph Waldo Emerson, "Self-Reliance," *Essays* (1841), full text available at https://archive.vcu.edu/english/engweb/transcendentalism/authors/emerson/essays/selfreliance.html.

49 Snyder, "7 Insights from Legendary Investor Warren Buffett."

50 "BP CEO Tony Hayward Apologizes for His Idiotic Statement: 'I'd like my life back.'" *Business Insider*, June 2, 2018, https://www.businessinsider.com/bp-ceo-tony-hayward-apologizes-for-saying-id-like-my-life-back-2010-6.

51   Ocean Conservancy, "Remembering the 9th Anniversary of the Deepwater Horizon
     Oil Disaster," April 15, 2019, https://oceanconservancy.org/blog/2019/04/15/
     remembering-9th-anniversary-deepwater-horizon-oil-disaster/.

CHAPTER 3

52   U.S. Food & Drug Administration, "Recalls, Market Withdrawals, and Safety Alerts," accessed August 24, 2016,
     https://www.fda.gov/safety/recalls-market-withdrawals-safety-alerts.

53   Tyco Integrated Security, "Recall: The Food Industry's Biggest Threat to
     Profitability," *Food Safety Magazine*, October 11, 2012, https://www.food-safety.com/
     articles/2542-recall-the-food-industrys-biggest-threat-to-profitability.

54   Harry Wood, "The Cost of Product Recalls to Food Businesses," Rentokil, July 11, 2017, https://www.rentokil.
     com/blog/industry-insights/cost-of-product-recalls.

55   Tyco Integrated Security, "Recall: The Food Industry's Biggest Threat to Profitability."

56   Timothy McLaughlin and P. J. Huffstutter, "Meat Packer Blames ABC's 'Pink Slime' for Nearly Killing
     Company," Reuters, June 5, 2017, https://www.reuters.com/article/us-abc-pinkslime-idUSKBN18W0KJ/.

57   Michael Moss, "Safety of Beef Processing Method Is Questioned," *New York Times*, December 30, 2009,
     https://www.nytimes.com/2009/12/31/us/31meat.html.

58   Reuters, "ABC Settles 'Pink Slime' Defamation Lawsuit," *Fortune*, June 28, 2017, https://fortune.
     com/2017/06/28/abcs-pink-slime-lawsuit-settled.

59   Jonathan Stempel, "AIG Sues Disney to Avoid Paying 'Pink Slim' Settlement Cost," Reuters, October 26,
     2017, https://www.reuters.com/article/us-walt-disney-pink-%20slime-aig/aig-sues-disney-to-avoid-
     paying-pink-slime-settle-%20ment-costs-idUSKBN1CV3FK/; Amanda Radke, "Disney Sued by AIG to
     Avoid Paying BPI Settlement," *Beef Magazine*, November 6, 2017, https://www.beefmagazine.com/outlook/
     disney-sued-aig-avoid-paying-bpi-settlement.

60   Joel Achenbach, "Why Do Many Reasonable People Doubt Science?" *National Geographic
     Magazine*, March 2015, https://www.nationalgeographic.com/magazine/article/
     science-doubters-climate-change-vaccinations-gmos.

61   Brian Kennedy and Alec Tyson, "Americans' Trust in Scientists, Positive Views of Science Continue to
     Decline," Pew Research Center, November 14, 2023, https://www.pewresearch.org/science/2023/11/14/
     americans-trust-in-scientists-positive-views-of-science-continue-to-decline/.

62   Tim Berners-Lee, "The World Wide Web: Past, Present and Future," August 1996, https://www.w3.org/People/
     Berners-Lee/1996/ppf.html.

63   "Iowa Tornado Outbreak—Nov. 9, 1975," KWWL.com, accessed August 25, 2019. https://addins.kwwl.com/
     blogs/weather/2017/11/iowa-tornado-outbreak-nov-9-1975.

64   George J. Siomkos and Gary Kurzbard, "The Hidden Crisis in Product-Harm Crisis Management," *European
     Journal of Marketing* 28, no. 2 (1994): 30–41, https://doi.org/10.1108/03090569410055265.

65   Jennifer L. Aaker et al., "When Good Brands Do Bad," *Journal of Consumer Research* 1, no. 1 (November 2004):
     1–16, https://doi.org/10.1086/383419; Rohini Ahluwalia et al., "Consumer Response to Negative Publicity: The
     Moderating Role of Commitment," *Journal of Marketing Research* 37, no. 2 (May 2000): 203–214, https://doi.
     org/10.1509/jmkr.37.2.203.18734.

66   Laura Olkkonen and Vilma Luomaaho. "Public Relations as Expectation Management," *Journal of
     Communication Management* 18, no. 3 (July 2014): 222–239, https://doi.org/10.1108/JCOM-02-2013-0012.

67   Vani Hari, "About Vani Hari," Food Babe, accessed September 8, 2019, https://foodbabe.com/about-me.

68   Susan Wong, "Impossible Foods' Plant-Based Meat Praised at CES 2019," Capital Lifestyle, January 28, 2019, https://www.capitalfm.co.ke/lifestyle/2019/01/28/food-technology-impossible-foods-next-generation-plant-based-meat-praised-at-ces-2019/.

69   Molly Wood, "Investors are Hungry for Meat-Replacement Technologies," Marketplace, February 4, 2019, https://www.marketplace.org/story/2019/02/04/investors-are-hungry-meat-replacement-technologies.

70   CNBC, "Why Beyond Meat and The Plant-Based Meat Industry Couldn't Live Up To The Hype," YouTube video, March 9, 2025, https://www.youtube.com/watch?v=GGNkHrNlIoI.

CHAPTER 4

71   Coletti, *Critical Moments*, 152.

72   James F. Haggerty, *Chief Crisis Officer: Structure and Leadership for Effective Communications Response* (Hart + Harvest, 2023), 45.

73   Dezenhall, *Glass Jaw*, 157.

74   Peter Stanton, *The Book of Crisis Management Strategies & Tactics* (PR News, Access Intelligence, 2017).

75   Richard S. Levick and Larry Smith, *Stop the Presses: The Crisis and Litigation PR Desk Reference* (Watershed Press, 2007).

76   Haggerty, *Chief Crisis Officer*, 34–35.

77   Mike Berardino, "Mike Tyson Explains One of His Most Famous Quotes," *South Florida Sun Sentinel*, November 9, 2012, https://www.sun-sentinel.com/2012/11/09/mike-tyson-explains-one-of-his-most-famous-quotes-3/.

78   Levick and Smith, *Stop the Presses*, 30–33.

79   Colin Dwyer, "Why the Delay Correcting False Alert? Hawaii Governor Forgot Twitter Password," NPR, January 23, 2018, https://www.npr.org/sections/thetwoway/2018/01/23/580058179/why-the-delay-correcting-false-alert-hawaii-governor-forgot-twitter-password.

CHAPTER 5

80   Alex Horton, "Coffee with Viagra-Like Ingredient Recalled after FDA Discovery," *Washington Post*, July 20, 2017, https://www.washingtonpost.com/news/to-your-health/wp/2017/07/20/coffee-with-viagra-like-ingredient-recalled-after-fda-discovery/.

81   CBS 8 Staff, "California Consumers Sue Boar's Head over Unsanitary Conditions and False Advertisement," CBS 8, March 14, 2025, https://www.cbs8.com/article/news/local/california-consumers-sue-boars-head-over-unsanitary-conditions-false-advertisement/509-ee9a3455-090a-4d0d-8528-c07b892bdacc.

82   Schema Design and Google Trends, "The Lifespan of News Stories: How the News Enters and Exits the Public Consciousness," accessed September 14, 2019, https://www.newslifespan.com.

83   Ashley Lutz, "These 6 Corporations Control 90% of the Media in America," *Business Insider*, June 14, 2012, https://www.businessinsider.com/these-6-corporations-control-90-of-the-media-in-america-2012-6.

84   Adam Hochberg, "Conan's Comedy Bit Hints at Serious Issues for Local TV News," Poynter, January 1, 2014, https://www.poynter.org/reporting-editing/2014/conans-comedy-bit-hints-at-serious-issues-for-local-tv-news.

85   Jane E. Dutton, "The Processing of Crisis and Non-Crisis Strategic Issues," *Journal of Management Studies* 23, no. 5 (September 1986): 502, https://doi.org/10.1111/j.1467-6486.1986.tb00434.x.

86   Keith Michael Hearit, "Mistakes were Made: Organizations, Apologia, and Crises of Social Legitimacy," *Communications Studies* 46, no. 1–2 (1995): 1–17, https://doi.org/10.1080/10510979509368435.

87   William L. Benoit, *Accounts, Excuses, and Apologies: Image Repair Theory and Research*, 2nd ed. (State University of New York Press, 2014).

88   Dan Millar and Larry Smith, *Crisis Management and Communication: How to Gain and Maintain Control*, 2nd ed. (International Association of Business Communicators, 2002), 1.

89   Coombs, *Ongoing Crisis Communication*, 3.

90   Dezenhall, *Glass Jaw*, 15.

91   Dezenhall, *Glass Jaw*, 27.

92   Niraj Chokshi, "That Wasn't Mark Twain: How a Misquotation is Born" *New York Times*, April 26, 2017, https://www.nytimes.com/2017/04/26/books/famous-misquotations.html.

93   Alexander Burns and Mike Allen, "The Art of the Tick-Tock," Politico, December 6, 2009, https://www.politico.com/story/2009/12/the-art-of-the-tick-tock-030248.

94   Forbes Agency Council, "Thirteen Golden Rules of PR Crisis Management," *Forbes*, January 20, 2017, https://www.forbes.com/sites/forbesagencycouncil/2017/06/20/13-golden-rules-of-pr-crisis-management/.

95   Haggerty, *Chief Crisis Officer*, 6.

96   Christopher Lehane et al., *Masters of Disaster: The Ten Commandments of Damage Control* (St. Martin's Press, 2024), 53.

97   Frederick B. Rogers et al., "The Golden Hour in Trauma: Dogma or Medical Folklore?," *The Journal of Lancaster General Hospital* 9, no. 1 (Spring 2014): 525–527, https://doi.org/10.1016/j.injury.2014.08.043.

98   Ralph Ellis, "Experts Say There Were Similarities in the Ethiopian Airlines and the Lion Air Crashes. What Were They?," CNN, April 4, 2019, https://www.cnn.com/2019/03/18/world/boeing-737-crashes-similarities/index.html.

99   Brooke Sutherland, "Boeing and the FAA Already Lost Control of the Narrative," Bloomberg, March 13, 2019, https://www.bloomberg.com/opinion/articles/2019-03-13/boeing-and-the-faa-737-max-grounding-damage-is-already?embedded-checkout=true.

100   "*E. coli* Outbreak Linked to Onions Served at McDonald's," Centers for Disease Control and Prevention, December 3, 2024, https://www.cdc.gov/ecoli/outbreaks/e-coli-O157.html.

101   Jordan Valinsky, "McDonald's Spends $100 Million to Lure Customers Back after *E. coli* Outbreak," CNN, November 15, 2024, https://www.cnn.com/2024/11/15/food/mcdonalds-marketing-money-e-coli.

102   Elisa Shearer and Katerina Eva Matsa, "News Use Across Social Media Platforms 2018," September 10, 2018, https://www.pewresearch.org/journalism/2018/09/10/news-use-across-social-media-platforms-2018/.

103   Molly Wood, "Social Media as Breaking-News Feed: Worse Information, Faster," CNet, April 19, 2013, https://www.cnet.com/culture/social-media-as-breaking-news-feed-worse-information-faster/.

104   Soroush Vosoughi et al., "The Spread of True and False News Online," *Science* 359, no. 6380 (March 2018): 1146–1151, https://doi.org/10.1126/science.aap9559.

105   Coombs, *Ongoing Crisis Communication*, 132.

106   Jenna Seter, "How PR Crises Impact Brand Reputation," Clutch, updated January 2, 2025, https://clutch.co/pr-firms/resources/how-pr-crises-impact-brand-reputation.

107 Seth Arenstein, "Rapid-Response Tactics for When the News About Your Organization is Bad and Getting Worse," in *Crisis Management Special Report*, PR News, July 25, 2016, https://www.prnewsonline.com/wp-content/uploads/2016/05/29007-PR-News_Crisis-Management-Special-Report-4.pdf.

108 Hearit, "Mistakes Were Made," 11.

CHAPTER 6

109 Kathleen M. Kowalski and Charles Vaught. "Judgment and Decision-Making Under Stress: An Overview for Emergency Managers," CDC Stacks Public Health Publications, 2008, https://stacks.cdc.gov/view/cdc/9732, 2.

110 Jennifer Schmidt et al., "The Scarcity Trap: Why We Keep Digging When We're Stuck in a Hole, *Hidden Brain*, NPR April 2, 2018, https://www.npr.org/2018/04/02/598119170/the-scarcity-trap-why-we-keep-digging-when-were-stuck-in-a-hole.

111 Tiffany O'Callaghan, "Psychologist: Why We Screw Up When the Heat Is On," *New Scientist*, July 6, 2011, https://www.newscientist.com/article/mg21128200-200-psychologist-why-we-screw-up-when-the-heat-is-on/.

CHAPTER 7

112 W. Timothy Coombs, "Choosing the Right Words: The Development of Guidelines for the Selection of the 'Appropriate' Crisis-Response Strategies," *Management Communication Quarterly* 8, no. 4 (May 1995), https://doi.org/10.1177/0893318995008004003.

113 Howard S. Becker, *Outsiders: Studies in the Sociology of Deviance* (Free Press, 1963).

114 Coombs, "Choosing the Right Words," 455.

115 Coca-Cola Company, "Veteran Employees Remember Infamous 1985 Launch of New Coke," Coca-Cola Company, https://www.coca-colacompany.com/about-us/history/the-infamous-1985-launch-of-new-coke.

116 Beatrice Christofaro, Beatrice, "Woman Dies in Meat Grinder Accident at Factory in Pennsylvania," *Business Insider*, April 25, 2019, https://www.businessinsider.com/woman-dies-in-meat-grinder-accident-jill-greninger-2019-4.

117 Keith M. Hearit, *Crisis Management by Apology: Corporate Responses to Allegations of Wrongdoing* (Lawrence Erlbaum Associates, 2006), 2.

118 Colin Pope, "Food Company Sued over Worker's Death," *Austin Business Journal*, July 20, 2003, https://www.bizjournals.com/austin/stories/2003/07/21/story4.html.

119 "Samuel Bankman-Fried Sentenced to 25 Years for His Orchestration of Multiple Fraudulent Schemes," U.S. Department of Justice, news release, March 28, 2024, https://www.justice.gov/archives/opa/pr/samuel-bankman-fried-sentenced-25-years-his-orchestration-multiple-fraudulent-schemes.

120 Coombs, "Choosing the Right Words," 457.

121 Tom Fanning and Jen Easterly, "The Attack on Colonial Pipeline: What We've Learned and What We've Done over the Past Two Years" Cybersecurity and Infrastructure Security Agency (CISA), news release, May 7, 2023, https://www.cisa.gov/news-events/news/attack-colonial-pipeline-what-weve-learned-what-weve-done-over-past-two-years.

122 Matthew Stabley, "Virginia Declares State of Emergency after Colonial Pipeline Cyberattack," NBC4 Washington, May 11, 2021, https://www.nbcwashington.com/news/local/virginia-declares-state-of-emergency-after-colonial-pipeline-cyberattack/2668526/.

123 Nell Henderson, "Gerber's Stand is Debated," *Washington Post*, March 2, 1986, https://www.washingtonpost.com/archive/business/1986/03/02/gerbers-stand-is-debated/c52f0bc2-c8d1-41ad-989b-1ddfccc0f5ba/.

CHAPTER 8

124 Fink, *Crisis Communications*, 249–251.

125 Mary Kay Ash, *Mary Kay on People Management* (Grand Central Publishing, 1984).

126 Daniel H. Pink, *When: The Scientific Secrets of Perfect Timing* (Riverhead Books, 2018), 160.

127 Jena McGregor, "The Best Time of Day—and Year—to Work Most Effectively," *Washington Post*, January 4, 2018, https://www.washingtonpost.com/news/on-leadership/wp/2018/01/04/the-best-time-of-day-and-year-to-work-most-effectively/.

128 Jeff Ansell, *When the Headline is You: An Insider's Guide to Handling the Media* (Jossey Bass Publishers, 2010), 62–64.

129 Benoit, *Accounts, Excuses, and Apologies*, 31.

130 Ana Swanson, "Kurt Vonnegut Graphed the World's Most Popular Stories," *Washington Post*, February 9, 2015, https://www.washingtonpost.com/news/wonk/wp/2015/02/09/kurt-vonnegut-graphed-the-worlds-most-popular-stories/.

131 Jon Fusco, "What Are the 6 Emotional Story Arcs?," No Film School, November 29, 2016, https://nofilmschool.com/2016/11/emotional-arcs-6-storytelling-kurt-vonnegut.

132 Amanda, "Ott and Aoki (2002), 'The Politics of Negotiating Public Tragedy,'" Comps Prep, August 12, 2013, http://edgarcomps.blogspot.com/2013/08/ott-and-aoki-2002-politics-of.html; Brian L. Ott and Eric Aoki, "The Politics of Negotiating Public Tragedy: Media Framing of the Matthew Shepard Murder," *Rhetoric and Public Affairs* 5, no. 3 (Fall 2002): 483–505, https://www.jstor.org/stable/41939768.

133 Charlie Campbell, *Scapegoat: A History of Blaming Other People* (Harry N. Abrams, 2012).

134 Carol Tavris and Elliot Aronson, *Mistakes Were Made (But Not by Me): Why We Justify Foolish Beliefs, Bad Decisions, and Hurtful Acts* (Houghton Mifflin Harcourt, 2007).

135 Josephine Campbell, "2021 Texas Power Crisis," Research Starters: Power and Energy, EBSCO, 2024, https://www.ebsco.com/research-starters/power-and-energy/2021-texas-power-crisis.

136 Peter Weber, "Texas Governor Walks Back Fox News Comments on Green New Deal, Says Gas, Coal Failed in Texas Freeze," The Week, February 18, 2021, https://theweek.com/speedreads/967540/texas-governor-walks-back-fox-news-comments-green-new-deal-says-gas-coal-failed-texas-freeze.

137 Benoit, *Accounts, Excuses, and Apologies*, 24.

138 Herbert McGann, "McDonald's Settles Beef Over Fries." CBS News, June 5, 2002, https://www.cbsnews.com/news/mcdonalds-settles-beef-over-fries.

139 "Fat Flap at McDonald's," CNN Money, May 3, 2001, archived at https://web.archive.org/web/20101009122058/http://money.cnn.com/2001/05/03/news/mcdonalds/.

140 Kristina Monllos, "Bud Light Says It 'Missed the Mark' With Line about 'Removing No from Your Vocabulary,'" AdWeek. April 28, 2015, https://www.adweek.com/brand-marketing/bud-light-says-it-missed-mark-tagline-about-removing-no-your-vocabulary-164374/.

141 Katie Reilly, "Tyson Recalls Nearly 12 Million Pounds of Chicken Strips Because They Might Contain Metal," *Time*, May 26, 2019, https://time.com/5583751/tyson-chicken-strip-recall.

142 Brenna Houck and Dana Hatic, "Why Does It Seem Like Everyone Is Getting Sick from Salad?," *Eater*, November 20, 2018, https://www.eater.com/2018/8/2/17639564/food-poisoning-foodborne-illness-trader-joes-chipotle.

143 Julia Belluz, "How Salad Became a Major Source of Food Poisoning in the US," Vox, May 18, 2018, https://www.vox.com/science-and-health/2018/4/26/17282378/romaine-lettuce-recall-ecoli-yuma.

144 Kevin Flower and Debra Goldschmidt, "365 People Sickened in McDonald's Salad Outbreak," CNN, August 2, 2018, https://www.cnn.com/2018/08/02/health/395-people-sickened-in-mcdonalds-salad-outbreak/index.html.

145 Jessi Hirsch, "Grower Steps to Keep Romaine Safe May Not Be Enough," Consumer Reports, February 8, 2019, https://www.consumerreports.org/food-safety/what-growers-are-doing-to-keep-romaine-lettuce-safe-to-eat.

146 Benoit, *Accounts, Excuses, and Apologies*, 42.

147 Mark Forsyth, *The Elements of Eloquence: How to Turn the Perfect English Phrase*, (Icon Books, 2016), 87.

148 Christopher Booker, *The Seven Basic Plots: Why We Tell Stories*, (Continuum International Publishing, 2005), 231.

149 Julia Jones, "A Taco Truck Served ICE Workers, Apologized, Then Apologized Again," CNN, October 29, 2019, https://www.cnn.com/2019/10/29/us/ice-taco-truck-trnd/index.html.

150 Benoit, *Accounts, Excuses, and Apologies*, 26.

151 Nicholas Tavuchis, *Mea Culpa: A Social Apology and Reconciliation*, (Stanford University Press, 1993), 20.

152 Ameeta Patel and Lamar Reinsch, "Companies Can Apologize: Corporate Apologies and Legal Liability," *Business and Professional Communication Quarterly* 66, no. 1 (March 2003): 9–25, https://doi.org/10.1177/108056990306600103; Lauren M. Bloom, *Art of the Apology: How, When, and Why to Give and Accept Apologies* (Fine & Kahn, 2014), 23–32.

153 Eric Dezenhall and John Weber, *Damage Control: The Essential Lessons of Crisis Management* (Prospecta Press, 2011), 81.

154 Nicolaus Mills, "The New Culture of Apology," *Dissent*, Fall 2001, https://www.dissentmagazine.org/article/the-new-culture-of-apology.

155 Bloom, *Art of the Apology*, 79.

156 Patel and Reinsch, "Companies Can Apologize," 17.

157 Elizabeth Latif, "Apologetic Justice: Evaluating Apologies Tailored toward Legal Solutions," *Boston University Law Review* 81, no.1 (February 2001): 289–320, https://heinonline.org/HOL/LandingPage?handle=hein.journals/bulr81&div=15&id=&page; Jonathan R. Cohen "Advising Clients to Apologize," *Southern California Law Review* 72 (May 1999): 1009–1070, http://scholarship.law.ufl.edu/facultypub/648.

158 Andy Simmons, "Here's What Really Happened in McDonald's Hot Coffee Lawsuit," *Reader's Digest*, updated June 9, 2025, https://www.rd.com/culture/hot-coffee-lawsuit; Bloom, *Art of the Apology*, 84.

159 W. Timothy Coombs and Sherry J. Holladay, "Comparing Apology to Equivalent Crisis Response Strategies: Clarifying Apology's Role and Value in Crisis Communication," *Public Relations Review* 34, no. 3 (September 2008): 252–257, https://doi.org/10.1016/j.pubrev.2008.04.001.

160 Edwin L. Battistella, *Sorry About That: The Language of Public Apology*, (Oxford University Press, 2014).

161 U.S. Department of Transportation, "DOT Penalizes Southwest Airlines $140 Million for 2022 Holiday Meltdown," news release, December 18, 2023, https://www.transportation.gov/briefing-room/dot-penalizes-southwest-airlines-140-million-2022-holiday-meltdown.

162 Niraj Chokshi and Peter Eavis, "Southwest's Meltdown Could Cost It Up to $825 Million," *New York Times,* January 6, 2023, https://www.nytimes.com/2023/01/06/business/southwest-airlines-meltdown-costs-reimbursement.html.

163 Charles Miller, "Exploring Southwest Airlines' Unique Point-to-Point Hub System and Fleet," *AirGuide,* September 16, 2023, https://airguide.info/exploring-southwest-airlines-unique-point-to-point-system-and-hubs/.

164 Joel Rose, "Southwest Will Pay a $140 Million Fine for Its Meltdown During the 2022 Holidays," NPR, December 18, 2023, https://www.npr.org/2023/12/18/1219906471/southwest-airlines-2022-meltdown-fined-faa.

165 *Good Morning America,* "Southwest CEO apologizes to customers, employees: 'There will be a lot of…'" Facebook Reels, December 30, 2022, https://www.facebook.com/watch/?v=2125016444359514.

166 Thomas H. Davenport and John C. Beck, *The Attention Economy: Understanding the New Currency of Business* (Harvard Business Review Press, 2002), 3.

167 Ansell, *When the Headline Is You,* 76–77.

168 Dana Liebelson, "Behind the Burrito: 5 Things Chipotle's Ads Don't Tell You," *Mother Jones,* September 25, 2013, https://www.motherjones.com/politics/2013/09/chipotle-commercial-sustainable-food-truth.

169 Chipotle, "Chipotle—Back to the Start," True Food Alliance, YouTube video, 2:19, September 18, 2013, accessed October 13, 2025, https://www.youtube.com/watch?v=S1zXGWK_knQ&list=RDS1zXGWK_knQ&start_radio=1.

170 Chipotle, "Chipotle: The Scarecrow," Ed Owen, YouTube video, 2:33, June 23, 2014, accessed September 26, 2019, https://www.youtube.com/watch?v=UQXPVZLBKLg.

171 Renu Singh, "How McDonald's and Wendy's are Copying Chipotle's Playbook," The Motley Fool, May 19, 2014, https://www.fool.com/investing/general/2014/05/19/how-mcdonalds-and-wendys-are-copying-chipotles-pla.aspx.

172 Tyler Barnett and Bethan Cianciolo, "Chipotle Knows What It's Doing by Closing Its Stores," *Fortune,* February 10, 2016, https://fortune.com/2016/02/10/chipotle-temporarily-closing-pr.

173 JoNel Aleccia, "Seattle Man Sues Chipotle; Fell Ill Months Before Big Outbreak," *Seattle Times,* January 11, 2016, https://www.seattletimes.com/seattle-news/health/seattle-man-sues-chipotle-fell-ill-months-before-big-outbreak/.

174 Minnesota Department of Health, "Health Officials Investigating Salmonella Cases Linked to Chipotle Restaurants in Minnesota," news release, September 10, 2015, published by *Mankato Free Press,* https://www.mankatofreepress.com/news/local_news/health-officials-investigating-salmonella-cases-linked-to-chipotle-restaurants-in-minnesota/article_6234e736-5802-11e5-bb27-b746c0312232.html.

175 "Chipotle Linked to Salmonella Outbreak in Minnesota, Health Officials Say, Prompting Investigation." ABC News, September 11, 2015, https://abcnews.go.com/Health/chipotle-linked-salmonel-la-outbreak-minnesota-health-officials-prompting/story?id=33691249.

176 Dan Flynn, "Chipotle's Bad Tomatoes Came from Nation's Largest Field Producer," Food Safety News, October 16, 2015, https://www.foodsafetynews.com/2015/10/chipotles-bad-tomatoes-came-from-nations-largest-field-producer.

177 Ransdell Pierson and Lisa Baertlein, "Chipotle Shuts Seattle, Portland Stores after E. Coli Outbreak," Reuters, November 1, 2015, https://www.reuters.com/article/business/chipotle-shuts-seattle-portland-stores-after-e-coli-outbreak-idUSKCN0SQ2CD/.

178 Elisha Fieldstadt, "43 Washington and Oregon Chipotle Restaurants Closed After *E. coli* Outbreak," ABC News, October 31, 2015, https://www.nbcnews.com/news/us-news/43-washington-oregon-chipotle-restaurants-closed-after-e-coli-outbreak-n455166.

179 Pierson and Baertlein, "Chipotle Shuts Seattle, Portland Stores"; "Chipotle Moves Aggressively to Address Issues in Washington and Oregon," Restaurant News, November 3, 2015, https://www.restaurantnews.com/chipotle-moves-aggressively-to-address-issues-in-washington-and-oregon/.

180 Candace Choi, "*E. coli* Outbreak Linked to Chipotle Expands to 6 States," Food Manufacturing, November 21, 2015, https://www.foodmanufacturing.com/ingredients/news/13182117/e-coli-outbreak-linked-to-chipotle-expands-to-6-states.

181 Hayley Peterson, "Chipotle: We're Taking 'Aggressive Steps' to Attack *E.coli*," *Business Insider*, November 20, 2015, https://www.businessinsider.com/chipotle-statement-e-coli-outbreak-2015-11.

182 "Chipotle Commits to Become Industry Leader in Food Safety," Perishable News, December 8, 2015, https://perishablenews.com/retailfoodservice/chipotle-commits-to-become-industry-leader-in-food-safety/.

183 Candace Choi, "Chipotle Tightens Food Safety as *E. coli* Outbreak Expands," KATU 2 ABC, December 4, 2015, https://katu.com/news/health/chipotle-tightens-food-safety-as-e-coli-outbreak-expands.

184 Choi, "Chipotle Tightens Food Safety as *E. coli* Outbreak Expands."

185 Katie Little, "Norovirus Confirmed in Boston Chipotle Outbreak, 120 sick," CNBC, December 9, 2015, https://www.cnbc.com/2015/12/09/norovirus-confirmed-in-boston-chipotle-outbreak-120-sick-dj.html.

186 Scott Stump, "Chipotle CEO Speaks Out After Health Scares: 'This Will Be the Safest Place to Eat,'" *Today*, December 10, 2015, https://www.today.com/news/chipotle-ceo-speaks-out-after-health-scares-will-be-safest-t60746.

187 Polly Mosendz, "Chipotle *E. coli* Outbreak Spreads Across Three More States," *Newsweek*, December 22, 2015, https://www.newsweek.com/chipotle-e-coli-outbreak-spreads-across-three-more-states-408222.

188 Stump, "Chipotle CEO Speaks Out After Health Scares," *Today*.

189 Sarah N. Lynch, "Chipotle Outbreak Eyed by Justice Dept. Consumer Unit," Reuters, January 8, 2016, https://www.reuters.com/article/us-chipotle-mexican-u-s-justice-dept/chipotle-outbreak-eyed-by-justice-dept-consumer-unit-idUSKBN0UM2GS20160108/.

190 Sarah Whitten, "CDC Declares Chipotle-Linked *E. coli* Outbreak Over," CNBC, February 1, 2016, https://www.cnbc.com/2016/02/01/cdc-declares-chipotle-linked-e-coli-outbreak-over.html.

191 Chipotle, "Chipotle Mexican Grill, Inc. Announces Fourth Quarter and Full Year 2015 Results; CDC Investigation Over; Chipotle Welcomes Customers Back to Restaurants," news release, February 2, 2016, https://ir.chipotle.com/news-releases?item=122452.

192 Sarah Whitten, "Chipotle's New Management Still Has the Same Old Problem: Food Safety," CNBC, July 31, 2018, https://www.cnbc.com/2018/07/31/chipotles-new-management-still-has-the-old-problem-food-safety.html/.

193 Chase Purdy, "After Its Food Safety Nightmare, People Are Eating at Chipotle Again," Quartz Media, April 25, 2017, https://qz.com/968286/chipotle-mexican-grill-cmg-burrito-chain-is-recovering-from-a-food-safety-scandal.

CHAPTER 9

194 Liz Calvario, "Astronomer Hires Gwyneth Paltrow as 'Temporary Spokesperson' After Coldplay Concert Scandal," Today, July 25, 2025, https://www.today.com/popculture/news/gwyneth-paltrow-astronomer-temporary-spokesperson-rcna221211.

195 Dezenhall and Weber, *Damage Control*, 177.

196 Centers for Disease Control and Prevention, *Crisis Emergency Risk Communication: Spokesperson*, updated 2014, accessed September 27, 2019, https://www.cdc.gov/cerc/media/pdfs/CERC_Spokesperson.pdf.

197 Brad Phillips, *The Media Training Bible: 101 Things You Absolutely, Positively Need to Know Before Your Next Interview* (SpeakGood Press, 2012).

198 Ben DiPietro, "When to Use the CEO as Crisis Spokesman," *Wall Street Journal*, January 26, 2018, https://blogs.wsj.com/riskandcompliance/2018/01/26/when-to-use-the-ceo-as-crisis-spokesman/.

199 Yvonne Raley, "Character Attacks: How to Properly Apply the Ad Hominem," *Scientific American* (June 2008), https://www.scientificamerican.com/article/character-attack/.

200 Chris Gidez and Mike Lawrence, "Should a CEO Be a Company's Primary Spokesperson During a Crisis?," PR Week, August 1, 2010, https://www.prweek.com/article/1266901/ceo-companys-primary-spokesperson-during-crisis.

201 Jane Freeman, "'Fair Terms and a Villain's Mind': Rhetorical Patterns in *The Merchant of Venice*," *Rhetorica: A Journal of the History of Rhetoric* 20, no. 2 (Spring 2002): 149–172, https://doi.org/10.1525/rh.2002.20.2.149.

202 "Marketing: Bud Light's Ill-Fated Campaign," The Week, May 6, 2023, https://theweek.com/business/1023244/marketing-bud-lights-ill-fated-campaign.

203 Amanda Holpuch, "Behind the Backlash against Bud Light," *New York Times*, November 21, 2023, https://www.nytimes.com/article/bud-light-boycott.html.

204 Harriet Alexander, "Bud Light Sales Tumble 26 Percent Amid Sobering Dylan Mulvaney Backlash—As Competitors See Spike in Beer Purchases," *Daily Mail*, May 2, 2023, https://www.dailymail.co.uk/news/article-12035697/Bud-Light-sales-26-PERCENT-compared-year-ago-amid-Dylan-Mulvaney-backlash.html.

205 Anson Frericks, "The Sad Saga of Bud Light," *The Free Press*, February 7, 2025, https://www.thefp.com/p/the-sad-saga-of-bud-light; Agustin Hays, "Bud Light Hasn't Recovered from Mulvaney Controversy, Ex-Anheuser-Busch Exec Says," Fox Business, February 7, 2025, https://www.foxbusiness.com/media/bud-light-hasnt-recovered-from-mulvaney-controversy-ex-anheuser-busch-exec-says.

206 Joseph A. Wulfsohn, "Critics Obliterate Anheuser-Busch CEO's 'Nothing' Statement amid Bud Light-Dylan Mulvaney Uproar: A 'Disaster,'" Fox News, April 14, 2023, https://www.foxnews.com/media/critics-obliterate-anheuser-busch-ceos-nothing-statement-amid-bud-light-dylan-mulvaney-uproar.

207 Megan Parris, "The Crowdstrike Update That Caused the Blue Screen of Death: What You Need to Know," Asgard Cyber Security, July 25, 2024, https://asgardcybersec.com/resources/blog/crowdstrike.

208 Matt Kapko, "Crowdstrike Says Flawed Update Was Live for 78 Minutes," Cybersecurity Dive, July 23, 2024, https://www.cybersecuritydive.com/news/crowdstrike-flawed-update-78-minutes/722070/.

209 George Kurtz, "July 19, 2024 Statement from Geroge Kurtz, Founder and CEO, Crowdstrike," "Remediation and Guidance Hub: Channel File 291 Incident," Crowdstrike, updated August 6, 2024. https://www.crowdstrike.com/falcon-content-update-remediation-and-guidance-hub/.

210 Carilu Dietrich, "Crowdstrike Crisis Comms Case Study," *Hypergrowth Leadership*, Substack, July 23, 2024, https://www.carilu.com/p/crowdstrike-crisis-comms-case-study.

211 David Weston, "Helping Our Customers through the CrowdStrike Outage," *Official Microsoft Blog*, Microsoft, July 20, 2024, https://blogs.microsoft.com/blog/2024/07/20/helping-our-customers-through-the-crowdstrike-outage/.

CHAPTER 10

212 Natalia Yannopoulou et al., "Media Amplification of a Brand Crisis and Its Effect on Brand Trust," *Journal of Marketing Management* 27, no. 5–6 (October 2010): 530–546, https://doi.org/10.1080/0267257X.2010.498141.

213 Daniel C. Hallin, "Sound Bite News: Television Coverage of Elections, 1968-1988," *Journal of Communication* 42, no. 2 (June 1992): 20, https://doi.org/10.1111/j.1460-2466.1992.tb00775.x.

214 Emma Rodero, "A Comparative Analysis of Speech Rate and Perceptions in Radio Bulletins," *Text & Talk: An Interdisciplinary Journal of Language Discourse Communication Studies* 32, no. 3 (May 2012):391–411, https://doi.org/10.1515/text-2012-0019.

215 Jo Craven McGinty, "Is Your Attention Span Shorter Than a Goldfish's?," *Wall Street Journal*, February 17, 2017, https://www.wsj.com/articles/is-your-attention-span-shorter-than-a-goldfishs-1487340000.

216 Lynne M. Sallot and Elizabeth Johnson Avery, "Investigating Relationships Between Journalists and Public Relations Practitioners: Working Together to Set, Frame and Build the Public Agenda, 1991-2004," *Public Relations Review* 32 no. 2 (June 2006): 151–159, https://doi.org/10.1016/j.pubrev.2006.02.008.

217 Joe Keohane, "What News-Writing Bots Mean for the Future of Journalism," *Wired*, February 16, 2017, https://www.wired.com/2017/02/robots-wrote-this-story/.

218 Orge Castellano, "The Future of Journalism: Will Robots Get It Right?," Medium, May 8, 2018, https://medium.com/@@orge/this-is-the-future-of-journalism-will-a-machine-get-it-right-d3e747f16751.

219 Dan McCue, "Newsroom Employment Continues to Decline, Led by Newspapers, Study Finds," *The Well News*, July 17, 2019, https://www.thewellnews.com/fourth-estate/newsroom-employment-continues-to-decline-led-by-newspapers-study-finds/.

220 McCue, "Newsroom Employment Continues to Decline"; Mary Yang, Vice Media, Once Worth $5.7 Billion, Files for Bankruptcy," NPR, May 15, 2023, https://www.npr.org/2023/05/15/1173260377/.

221 Andrew Gauthier, "25 Anchors Read the Exact Same Script," Adweek, July 18, 2012, https://www.adweek.com/tvspy/video-25-anchors-read-the-exact-same-script/55836/.

222 "Mindless Media Compilation: News Anchors Reading the Same Script," GoddamZooey, YouTube, May 11, 2013, accessed October 14, 2025, https://www.youtube.com/watch?v=PStpvviPgxk.

223 Team Coco, "Is It Time For Dogs To Have A Social Network Of Their Own?," YouTube, May 9, 2012, accessed September 29, 2019, https://www.youtube.com/watch?v=dZElSajQdOo.

224 Deborah Potter, "Cookie-Cutter News: As Local TV Operations Struggle to Fill More Hours of Programming, Syndicated Stories Are Showing Up on Local Newscasts Across the Country," *American Journalism Review* 35, no. 1 (Spring 2013).

225 David Henderson, *Making News: A Straight-Shooting Guide to Media Relations* (iUniverse Star, 2006), 63.

226 Andrew Tyndall, *The Anchor's Job, In Minute Detail* (Broadcasting & Cable, 2006), 136.

227 Tyndall, *The Anchor's Job*, 4.

228 Tyndall, *The Anchor's Job*, 68.

229 Michael Cavna, "RIP, United Media: A Century-Old Syndicate Closes Its Historic Doors," *Washington Post*, July 1, 2011, https://www.washingtonpost.com/blogs/comic-riffs/post/rip-united-media-a-century-old-syndicate-closes-its-historic-doors/2011/07/01/AGThVctH_blog.html; "Newspaper Syndicates: Staying Relevant," *Editor & Publisher* 147, no. 7 (July 2014): 30–36.

230 FrugalDad, "Media Consolidation: The Illusion of Choice (Graphic)," pub. David Wallace, Infographic Journal, June 15, 2012, accessed October 14, 2025, https://infographicjournal.com/media-consolidation-the-illusion-of-choice/.

231 Sally Stewart, *Media Training 101: A Guide to Meeting the Press* (Wiley, 2003), 16.

232 James L. Vance, "Media Interviews," *Law Enforcement Bulletin* 6, no. 2 (February 1997): 1–11, https://leb.fbi.gov/file-repository/archives/february-1997.pdf/view.

233 Isabel Wilkerson, "Interviewing Sources." *Nieman Reports* 56 no. 1 (March 2002): 16–17, https://niemanreports.org/articles/interviewing-sources/.

234 Kenneth Burke, *A Grammar of Motives* (University of California Press, 1969), xv–xxiii.

235 Tim Harrower, *Inside Reporting: A Practical Guide to the Craft of Journalism*, 3rd ed. (McGraw-Hill Higher Education, 2012) 3rd edition.

236 Ron Fournier, "In Defense of Gotcha Questions," *The Atlantic*, February 25, 2015, https://www.theatlantic.com/politics/archive/2015/02/in-defense-of-gotcha-questions/460743/.

237 Pew Research Center, "Writing Survey Questions," Pew Research Center, accessed October 14, 2025, https://www.pewresearch.org/writing-survey-questions/.

238 Norman M. Bradburn et al., *Asking Questions: The Definitive Guide to Questionnaire Design—For Market Research, Political Polls, and Social and Health Questionnaires*, 2nd ed. (Jossey-Bass, 2004), 142, 136.

239 "Leading Questions," Media College, Accessed October 1, 2019, https://www.mediacollege.com/journalism/interviews/leading-questions.html.

240 Melia Poler Kovacic and Karmen Erjavec, "Construction of Semi-Investigative Reporting," *Journalism Studies* 11, no. 3 (July 2010): 328–343, https://doi.org/10.1080/1461670X.2010.493321.

241 Pär-Anders Granhag et al., "Eliciting Intelligence with the Scharff Technique: Interviewing More and Less Cooperative and Capable Sources," *Psychology, Public Policy, and Law* 21, no. 1 (2015): 100–110, http://dx.doi.org/10.1037/law0000030.

242 Bradburn et al., *Asking Questions*, 136.

243 "Rhetorical question," Grammarist, accessed July 2019, https://grammarist.com/phrase/rhetorical-question/.

244 Alan Manning and Nicole Amare, "Bad News First: How Optimal Directness Depends on What Is Negated," paper presented at the 2017 IEEE International Professional Communication Conference (July 23–26, 2017), https://doi.org/10.1109/IPCC.2017.8013959.

CHAPTER 11

245 Manning and Amare, "Bad News First."

246 Marshall McLuhan, *Understanding Media: The Extensions of Man* (McGraw-Hill, 1974, repr., McGraw-Hill, 2013), 17.

247 Blue Bell Creameries, "Blue Bell CEO Apologizes," Grady Newsource, YouTube, 0:32, posted April 21, 2015, accessed August 28, 2019, https://www.youtube.com/watch?v=yphTqJmVD1A.

248 Blue Bell Creameries, "Blue Bell Ice Cream Commercial," Sharlene Rochen, YouTube, 0:35, posted June 26, 2012, accessed August 28, 2019, https://www.youtube.com/watch?v=TYBImTRh-zM.

249 Bill Marler, "A Blue Bell Listeria Timeline—2010 to 2015," *Marler Blog*, May 31, 2015, https://www.marlerblog.com/legal-cases/a-blue-bell-listeria-timeline-2010-to-2015/.

250 Centers for Disease Control and Prevention, "2015 Outbreak of *Listeria* Infections Linked to Blue Bell Creameries Products," CDC Archive, June 10, 2015, https://archive.cdc.gov/#/details?url=https://www.cdc.gov/listeria/outbreaks/ice-cream-03-15/index.html.

251 Peter Elkind, "How Ice Cream Maker Blue Bell Blew It," *Fortune*, September 25, 2015, https://fortune.com/2015/09/25/blue-bell-listeria-recall.

252 "3 Deaths, 5 Illnesses: Listeria Outbreak Linked to Single-Serving Blue Bell Ice Cream," Food Safety News, March 13, 2015, https://www.foodsafetynews.com/2015/03/3-deaths-5-illnesses-listeria-outbreak-linked-to-single-serving-blue-bell-ice-cream.

253 Olivia Pulsinelli, "Blue Bell Issues First Recall in 108 Years after Listeria Found," *Houston Business Journal*, March 13, 2015, https://www.bizjournals.com/houston/news/2015/03/13/blue-bell-products-recalled-three-deaths-reported.html.

254 "Blue Bell Issues First Recall in 108 Years," Fox23 News, March 13, 2015, https://www.fox23.com/news/local/blue-bell-issues-first-recall-in-108-years/article_cf95f10a-3b77-5bd4-ba11-5d37faddd669.html.

255 Roy Wenzel and Kelsey Ryan, "3 Kansans Die after Eating Listeria-Contaminated Blue Bell Ice Cream, State Says," *Wichita Eagle*, March 13, 2015, https://www.kansas.com/news/state/article14037434.html.

256 Carla Gillespie, "Blue Bell Ice Cream Listeria Outbreak Timeline," Food Poisoning Bulletin, August 28, 2015, https://foodpoisoningbulletin.com/2015/blue-bell-ice-cream-listeria-outbreak-timeline.

257 Olivia Pulsinelli, "Blue Bell Issues Another Recall Related to Listeria," *Houston Business Journal*, March 24, 2015, https://www.bizjournals.com/houston/news/2015/03/24/blue-bell-issues-another-recall-related-to.html.

258 Centers for Disease Control and Prevention, "2015 Outbreak of *Listeria* Infections."

259 Centers for Disease Control and Prevention, "2015 Outbreak of *Listeria* Infections."

260 Centers for Disease Control and Prevention, "2015 Outbreak of *Listeria* Infections."

261 Centers for Disease Control and Prevention, "2015 Outbreak of *Listeria* Infections."

262 Centers for Disease Control and Prevention, "2015 Outbreak of *Listeria* Infections."

263 Gillespie, "Blue Bell Ice Cream Listeria Outbreak Timeline."

264 "Blue Bell Recalls Ice Cream Cups That Could Contain Listeria." CW33, March 25, 2015, https://cw33.com/2015/03/25/blue-bell-recalls-ice-cream-cups-that-could-contain-listeria.

265 Centers for Disease Control and Prevention, "2015 Outbreak of *Listeria* Infections."

266 Centers for Disease Control and Prevention, "2015 Outbreak of *Listeria* Infections."

267 Elkind, "How Ice Cream Maker Blue Bell Blew It."

268 Centers for Disease Control and Prevention, "2015 Outbreak of *Listeria* Infections."

269 Centers for Disease Control and Prevention, "2015 Outbreak of *Listeria* Infections."

270 Juan A. Lozano, "Blue Bell Suspending Operations at Okla. Plant," Chron, April 3, 2015, https://www.chron.com/business/article/Blue-Bell-suspending-operations-at-Okla-plant-6178252.php.

271 Centers for Disease Control and Prevention, "2015 Outbreak of *Listeria* Infections."

272 Gillespie, "Blue Bell Ice Cream Listeria Outbreak Timeline."

273 Centers for Disease Control and Prevention, "2015 Outbreak of *Listeria* Infections."

274 Centers for Disease Control and Prevention, "2015 Outbreak of *Listeria* Infections."

275 Centers for Disease Control and Prevention, "2015 Outbreak of *Listeria* Infections."

276 Chris Weinandt, "Blue Bell's Monday Statement on Latest Recall," *Dallas Morning News*, April 20, 2015, https://www.dallasnews.com/news/news/2015/04/20/blue-bell-s-monday-statement-on-latest-recall.

277 Brady Dennis, "Blue Bell Issues Nationwide Recall of All Products, as Listeria Outbreak Grows," *Washington Post*, April 20, 2015, https://www.washingtonpost.com/news/to-your-health/wp/2015/04/20/blue-bell-issues-nationwide-recall-of-all-products-over-listeria-worries/.

278 Centers for Disease Control and Prevention, "2015 Outbreak of *Listeria* Infections."

279 Centers for Disease Control and Prevention, "2015 Outbreak of *Listeria* Infections."

280 Gillespie, "Blue Bell Ice Cream Listeria Outbreak Timeline."

281 Gillespie, "Blue Bell Ice Cream Listeria Outbreak Timeline."

282 Mark Collette, "FDA: Blue Bell Knew of Listeria, Didn't Correct Problems," *Houston Chronicle*, May 7, 2015, https://www.houstonchronicle.com/news/houston-texas/houston/article/FDA-Blue-Bell-didn-t-correct-problems-after-6249881.php.

283 Centers for Disease Control and Prevention, "2015 Outbreak of *Listeria* Infections."

284 Collette, FDA: Blue Bell Knew of Listeria."

285 Collette, FDA: Blue Bell Knew of Listeria."

286 Tessa Berenson Rogers, "Blue Bell Knew About Listeria Contamination Two Years Ago, Feds Say," *Time*, May 8, 2015, https://time.com/3850863/blue-bell-listeria-fda.

287 Sarah McHaney, "Blue Bell Creameries Lays Off 1,450 Employees Due to Listeria Outbreak," PBS, May 15, 2015, https://www.pbs.org/newshour/nation/blue-bell-creameries-lays-1450-employees-due-listeria-outbreak.

288 Scott Noll, "Blue Bell Lays Off 1,450 Workers; 1,400 More Furloughed," *USA Today*, May 15, 2015, https://www.usatoday.com/story/money/business/2015/05/15/blue-bell-layoffs/27389163/.

289 Noll, "Blue Bell Lays Off 1,450 Workers."

290 Cathy Siegner,. "FDA Posts Blue Bell Inspection Reports from 2007–2014," Food Safety News, May 21, 2015, https://www.foodsafetynews.com/2015/05/fda-posts-blue-bell-inspection-reports-from-2007-2014.

291 Blue Bell Creameries, Inc., *Responses of Blue Bell Creameries, Inc., to FDA Form 483s*, Food and Drug Administration, May 22, 2015, https://www.fda.gov/media/92507/download.

292 Andrew Marton, "Sid Bass: Why the Fort Worth Billionaire saved Blue Bell," *Fort Worth Star Telegram*, October 31, 2015, https://www.star-telegram.com/news/business/article42097164.html.

293 Marton, "Sid Bass."

294 Associated Press, "Bass Lending $125 Million to Blue Bell," CBS News, July 17, 2015, https://www.cbsnews.com/texas/news/bass-lending-125-million-to-blue-bell/.

295 "Alabama Health Officials OK Production, Sale of Blue Bell Ice Cream," NBC 5 DFW, August 5, 2015, https://www.nbcdfw.com/news/local/alabama-health-officials-ok-production-sale-of-blue-bell-ice-cream/160374/.

296 Tiffany Wade, "Blue Bell Returns to Stores After Five Month Hiatus," *The Highlife*, Sept. 30, 2015, accessed August 24, 2019. Note: some of these materials are no longer available online. Validation of their former existence can also be found at: Michal Addady, "These Are the Areas Blue Bell Will Return to Starting August 31," August 17, 2015, https://fortune.com/2015/08/17/blue-bell-return/.

297 Associated Press, "Blue Bell resumes production at Oklahoma facility," *Detroit Free Press*, September 1, 2015, https://www.freep.com/story/money/business/2015/09/02/blue-bell-ice-cream/71564590.

298 Jerrod Kingery, "Blue Bell Reopens Brenham, Texas Plant," CBS Austin, https://cbsaustin.com/news/local/blue-bell-reopens-brenham-texas-plant.

299 Kingery, "Blue Bell Reopens Brenham, Texas Plant."

300 "The First Press Release," News Museum, accessed October 15, 2025, https://www.newsmuseum.pt/en/spin-wall/first-press-release.

301 Hannah Fleishman, "How to Write a Press Release [Free Press Release Template + Examples]," HubSpot Blog, July 30, 2024, https://blog.hubspot.com/marketing/bid-adieu-press-release-oe.

302 Myria Watkins Allen and Rachel H. Caillouet, "Legitimation Endeavors: Impression Management Strategies Used by an Organization in Crisis," Communication Monographs 61, no. 1 (June 2009): 44–62, https://doi.org/10.1080/03637759409376322; Christin M. Pearson and Ian I. Mitroff, "From Crisis Prone to Crisis Prepared: A Framework for Crisis Management," *The Executive* 7, no. 1 (February 1993): 48–59, https://www.jstor.org/stable/4165107.

303 "Dry, Dusty 1936," Iowa Pathways, Iowa PBS, accessed October 4, 2019, https://www.iowapbs.org/iowapathways/mypath/2706/dry-dusty-1936.

304 Everett M. Rogers, *Diffusion of Innovations*, 5th ed., (Free Press, 2003), 5.

305 Rogers, *Diffusion of Innovations*, 282–284.

306 Chris Maloney, "The Secret to Accelerating Diffusion of Innovation: The 16% Rule Explained," May 10, 2010, https://innovateordie.com.au/2010/05/10/the-secret-to-accelerating-diffusion-of-innovation-the-16-rule-explained/.

307 Krogerus and Tschäppeler, *The Decision Book*, 114–115.

308 Alex Lowy and Phil Hood, *The Power of the 2 x 2 Matrix: Using 2 x 2 Thinking to Solve Business Problems and Make Better Decisions* (Jossey-Bass Publishers, 2004).

309 Richard H. Thaler et al., "Choice Architecture," in *The Behavioral Foundations of Public Policy*, ed. Eldar Shafir, (Princeton University Press, 2012), 436.

310 Alisha Ebrahimji, "This Alaska Airlines Boeing Lost Its Door Plug in Flight. The Impact Ripped Headrests off Seats and a Shirt off a Passenger," CNN, January 8, 2024, https://www.cnn.com/2024/01/08/us/what-happened-alaska-airlines-flight-1282/index.html.

311 David Gelles, "Boeing 737 Max: What's Happened after the 2 Deadly Crashes," *New York Times*, October 28, 2019, https://www.nytimes.com/interactive/2019/business/boeing-737-crashes.html.

312 Michelle Wang and James Fitzpatrick, "How Good Was Boeing's Crisis Communication Response?," Crisis Shield, March 22, 2019, https://www.crisisshield.com.au/post/2019/03/22/how-good-was-boeings-crisis-communication-response.

313 "Lion Air Flight JT 610 Crash," Wisner Baum, October 29, 2018, https://www.wisnerbaum.com/blog/2018/october/lion-air-flight-jt-610-crash/.

314 Federal Aviation Administration, "Updates on Boeing 737-9 Max Aircraft," Federal Aviation Administration, December 5, 2024, https://www.faa.gov/newsroom/updates-boeing-737-9-max-aircraft; Caleb Revill, "Boeing Reports $11.8B Annual Loss in Q4 Earnings," *Flying Magazine*, January 28, 2025, https://www.flyingmag.com/boeing-reports-11-8b-annual-loss-in-q4-earnings.

315 Catherine Thorbecke, "Boeing CEO Acknowledges 'Mistake' Related to Terrifying Alaska Airlines Flight," CNN Business, January 10, 2024, https://www.cnn.com/2024/01/09/business/boeing-safety-meeting-737-max-factory.

316 Breck Dumas, "Boeing CEO 'Fought Back Tears' Addressing Employees after Alaska Air Incident," Fox Business, January 12, 2024, https://www.foxbusiness.com/markets/boeing-ceo-fought-back-tears-addressing-employees-after-alaska-air-incident.

317 Adam Fisher, "How Has Boeing Handled the Latest Blow to Its Reputation?," Media First: Specialists in Communication Training, January 16, 2024, https://www.mediafirst.co.uk/blog/how-has-boeing-handled-the-latest-blow-to-its-reputation.

318 "Anonymous Sources," Telling the Story, Associated Press Stylebook, accessed October 9, 2019, https://www.ap.org/about/news-values-and-principles/telling-the-story/anonymous-sources.

319 Daniel Kahneman, *Thinking, Fast and Slow* (Farrar, Straus & Giroux, 2011), 201.

320 Robin McDowel et al., "AP Investigation: Fish Billed as Local Isn't Always Local," Associated Press, June 15, 2018, https://apnews.com/73646ad2aaac4666a7124806b2e6a5bc.

321 Hearit, "Mistakes were Made," 11.

322 Cialdini, *Influence*, 218.

323 Aon, *Managing Risk: How to Maximize Performance in Volatile Times* (2019), https://www.aon.com/2019-global-risk-management-survey/index.html.

324 J. David Goodman, "Beryl Leaves Millions Without Power in Houston: What to Know," *New York Times*, July 9, 2024, https://www.nytimes.com/2024/07/09/us/beryl-storm-forecast.html.

325 Alejandra Martinez and Emily Foxhall, "Public Utility Commission Releases Investigative Report on CenterPoint Energy's Hurricane Beryl Response," *Texas Tribune*, July 25, 2024, https://www.texastribune.org/2024/07/25/texas-power-grid-puc-centerpoint-hurricane-beryl/; Jef Rouner, "CenterPoint Defends Response, but Questions Continue," *Reform Austin*, July 12, 2024, https://www.reformaustin.org/infrastructure/centerpoint-defends-response-but-questions-continue/.

326 Holly Galvan Posey, "CenterPoint CEO Faces Backlash over Photo amid Hurricane Beryl Recovery Efforts in Houston," Click2Houston, July 18, 2024, https://www.click2houston.com/news/local/2024/07/17/centerpoint-ceo-faces-backlash-over-photo-amid-hurricane-beryl-recovery-efforts-in-houston/.

327 Lisa Lupo, "Fresh Express Releases Interim Report on Cyclospora Outbreak Prevention," June 11, 2019, https://www.qualityassurancemag.com/news/fresh-express-releases-interim-report-on-cyclospora-outbreak-prevention/.

CHAPTER 12

328 Aneeq Zaheer, "Kingda Ka: The Thrill, the Records, and the Myth of Implosion," Geeks, accessed July 1, 2025, https://vocal.media/geeks/kingda-ka-the-thrill-the-records-and-the-myth-of-implosion.

329 "Energy Transformation on a Roller Coaster," The Physics Classroom, accessed July 1, 2025, https://www.physicsclassroom.com/mmedia/energy/ce.cfm.

330 Neil Culbertson and Laurel Kennedy, "In Times of Crisis, the CEO Becomes Chief Emergency Officer," Chief Executive, November 29, 2018, https://chiefexecutive.net/in-times-of-crisis-the-ceo-becomes-chief-emergency-officer/.

331 Brandon Drenon and Nadine Yousif, "What Has Sean 'Diddy' Combs Been Convicted Of?," BBC News, July 2, 2025, https://www.bbc.com/news/articles/c0qz32wzeego; Justin Klawans, "A Running List of Elon Musk's Biggest Controversies," The Week, June 11, 2025, https://theweek.com/elon-musk/1022182/elon-musks-most-controversial-moments; Krystie Lee Yandoli, "Ellen DeGeneres Is Ending Her TV Show after Allegations of Sexual Misconduct and a Toxic Workplace," BuzzFeed News, May 12, 2021, https://www.buzzfeednews.com/article/krystieyandoli/ellen-degeneres-show-ending; Amber Melville-Brown, "The Reputational Fallout of Depp v. Heard," *Wealth Management*, May 13, 2022, https://www.wealthmanagement.com/high-net-worth/the-reputational-fallout-of-depp-v-heard; "Kanye West Faces Legal Firestorm: Antisemitism, Nazi Claims, and Talent Agency Fallout Rock the Rapper," *The Economic Times*, February 12, 2025, https://economictimes.indiatimes.com/magazines/panache/kanye-west-faces-legal-firestorm-antisemitism-nazi-claims-and-talent-agency-fallout-rock-the-rapper/articleshow/118178248.cms?from=mdr.

332 "The Munger Operating System: A Life That Works," Farnam Street, accessed July 1, 2025. https://fs.blog/munger-operating-system/.

333 Murray S. Davis, "That's Interesting! Towards a Phenomenology of Sociology and a Sociology of Phenomenology," *Philosophy of Social Sciences*, 1 no. 4 (June 1971): 309–344, https://doi.org/10.1177/004839317100100211.

334 Edward Boches, "Bill Bernbach and the Beginning," Medium, May 26, 2014, https://medium.com/
    what-do-you-want-to-know/bill-bernbach-and-the-beginning-7e49c2242390.

335 "A Principle Isn't a Principle Until It Costs You Money," The Big Apple, October 13, 2016,
    accessed October 13, 2019, https://www.barrypopik.com/index.php/new_york_city/
    entry/a_principle_isnt_a_principle_until_it_costs_you_money.

336 Edelman, "Two Thirds of Consumers Worldwide Now Buy on Beliefs," news release, October 2, 2018, https://
    www.edelman.com/news-awards/two-thirds-consumers-worldwide-now-buy-beliefs.

337 Douglas Atkin, *The Culting of Brands: When Customers Become True Believers* (Penguin Group, 2004).

PROJET

D'ÉRIGER UN MONUMENT

A LA GLOIRE

DE L'EMPEREUR.

PAR A.-F. PEYRE,

DE L'INSTITUT NATIONAL.

[illegible]

[illegible]
[illegible]
[illegible]
[illegible]
[illegible]
[illegible]

MONUMENT

A

LA GLOIRE DE L'EMPEREUR.

Ce serait à cette époque à jamais mémorable où la Nation, reconnoissante des bienfaits de Napoléon Bonaparte, vient d'appeler ce Héros au gouvernement de l'Empire, que le Peuple français devrait ériger à ce Monarque un monument digne de sa gloire dans sa capitale, au centre de son palais, et rendre ce palais le plus magnifique qui ait jamais existé. Mais les dépenses que nécessite la guerre ne permettant pas de s'occuper de l'exécution de ce vaste projet, il faudrait la reporter au temps où ce Héros pacificateur aura vaincu le fier Anglais et donné la paix à l'Europe, lorsque sa bonté paternelle, continuant à s'étendre sur le commerce, sur les arts et sur l'agriculture, aura fait renaître avec éclat ces beaux jours dont nous avions vu paraître l'aurore.

Henri IV voulait réunir les Tuileries au Louvre. Déja il avait fait construire la galerie, aujourd'hui du Muséum. Louis XIV avait suivi ce projet; il avait fait

de grands travaux au Louvre, et commencé, du côté
des Tuileries, un bâtiment semblable à la galerie cons-
truite par Henri IV.

L'intention de ces grands hommes était de ne former
qu'une place dans cette vaste enceinte. Idée sublime!....

C'est sous l'empire de Napoléon le grand que cette
belle conception doit avoir son exécution ; et c'est au
centre de cette place magnifique qu'il faut ériger à ce
Monarque un monument aussi durable que sa gloire,
tel que la statue équestre de ce héros, élevée sur un
piédestal simple, embelli du récit de ses grandes actions.

Tous les Français devraient concourir à l'exécution
de ce grand édifice, en faisant chacun l'avance d'une
légère rétribution dont ils auraient l'espérance de retirer
un grand profit.

L'on formerait une loterie qui aurait trois ou six
tirages. Chaque Français en âge de travailler s'enga-
gerait à prendre une action dont la valeur égalerait une
journée ou une demi-journée de son travail, du produit
de son emploi ou de son revenu.

Cette loterie serait combinée de manière que la masse
des lots, dans la classe la moins fortunée, serait en
raison de la mise, comme 16 $\frac{3}{4}$ est à 25, et que le produit net pour les trois tirages, les lots et les frais pré-
levés, serait de *trois cents millions*.

On emploierait cette somme de trois cents millions à
acquérir les terrains nécessaires à former la place, à
construire des bâtimens du côté opposé à la galerie du
Muséum, qui agrandiraient le palais de l'Empereur, et
procureraient à ce prince de magnifiques appartemens,

qui pourraient contenir encore de beaux hôtels pour les grands officiers de l'Empire, sans empêcher la communication des appartemens de l'Empereur dans tout le pourtour de ce vaste édifice, et sans lui ôter l'avantage d'avoir dans son intérieur le Muséum et la Bibliothèque impériale : ce qui rendrait ce palais le plus vaste et le plus magnifique qu'on ait jamais connu.

Ce serait avec cette somme de trois cents millions qu'on érigerait au centre de cette place le monument élevé à la gloire de l'Empereur ; elle faciliterait en même temps les moyens d'amener à Paris les eaux qu'on se propose depuis long-temps d'y faire venir : ces eaux seraient d'un grand avantage pour la ville, et en procureraient abondamment à des fontaines toujours jaillissantes qu'on érigerait dans cette place.

Avec cette même somme de trois cents millions l'on embellirait la place de trophées et de statues de marbre ou de bronze.

On pratiquerait autour du monument érigé à la gloire de l'Empereur un cirque dans lequel seraient ces fontaines jaillissantes, semblables à celles qui concourent à embellir la place de Saint-Pierre à Rome, où les eaux de rivières entières s'élèvent en masse à la hauteur de trente-quatre pieds, et dont la chute a une circonférence de cinquante à soixante pieds. Les dimensions de ce cirque seraient de huit cents pieds de long sur environ quatre cent trente pieds de large.

L'on pratiquerait des deux côtés du cirque des allées dont celle du milieu aurait cent pieds, afin qu'un escadron puisse y passer au galop sur trente-deux ou trente-

six hommes de front ; elles seraient séparées du cirque
par des gradins et un stylobate sur lequel seraient placés
ces trophées et ces statues.

Aux extrémités du cirque, à l'entrée du palais des
Tuileries et du Louvre, seraient quatre colonnes triom-
phales qui supporteroient des fanaux pour éclairer la
place dans tous les temps.

Ce cirque et l'espace immense qui l'environne procureraient à l'Empereur la facilité de voir, des croisées de
son palais, manœuvrer peut-être trente mille hommes.

L'on pourrait célébrer chaque année dans cette place
l'anniversaire du couronnement de l'Empereur.

Les fêtes données dans ce beau local prendraient
toutes un grand caractère, et il serait possible de les
varier à l'infini. L'on pourrait, dans des temps, inonder
le cirque comme on inonde à Rome la place Navone ;
ce qui procurerait l'avantage de donner dans ce même
local des fêtes navales, et un spectacle semblable à celui
dont on jouit à Rome lors de ces inondations. Ce mé-
lange dans l'eau, de voitures, de cavaliers qui circu-
leraient entre des barques voguantes à pleines voiles ou
à force de rames, ce concours du public, la marche
tranquille des voitures dans les grandes allées, ce beau
fond formé par les palais dont l'architecture se marie-
rait avec la verdure des plantations, ces statues isolées,
ces différens plans du terrain, l'aspect de ces fontaines
jaillissantes dont la masse d'eau serait énorme, ce monument imposant au centre de cette place, cet ensemble,
rendraient ce spectacle infiniment plus grand et plus
intéressant que celui de l'inondation de la place Na-

vone, qui pourtant est citée comme une des curiosités de Rome.

Le Louvre réuni au palais impérial par cette place magnifique, ce superbe jardin des Tuileries qu'on doit lier avec les Champs-Élysées par des plantations, formeraient, avec cette promenade, un ensemble qui, jusqu'à la grande étoile, aurait près de deux lieues de longueur.

Avec cette somme de trois cents millions on pourrait encore terminer le projet, adopté par l'Empereur, pour l'arrivée du canal de l'Ourque ; la formation d'un port et d'une place sur le terrain de la Bastille, terminer le Panthéon français, le portail de Saint-Sulpice, construire la place qui précède cette église, achever des temples et des hospices commencés, faire enfin que cette ville déja superbe rivalise en magnificence avec l'ancienne capitale du monde.

En continuant cette loterie l'on pourrait embellir également toutes les villes de l'empire, y ériger des monumens et de superbes édifices. Ces travaux immenses, faits par la nation entière, deviendraient, pour la postérité la plus reculée, des preuves matérielles de la grandeur et de la puissance du premier Empereur des Français (1).

---

(1) L'on a souvent établi des loteries pour subvenir à la dépense de travaux publics. Le canal ouvert dans le royaume de Murcie en Espagne, vers l'an 1760, fut exécuté ainsi ; la chance étoit moins avantageuse, et les étrangers souscrivirent pour la majeure partie.

Le portail de Saint-Sulpice et celui de Sainte-Géneviève furent construits sur le produit des loteries dont on faisoit un tirage tous les mois. La valeur du billet était de vingt sols.

Projet de loterie établie sur la valeur d'une journée de travail.

En supposant que la population de la France soit exactement trente millions d'individus, il y en aurait au plus un tiers de contribuables ; savoir, les hommes en état de travailler depuis l'âge de dix-huit ans jusqu'à la fin de leur vie, et les femmes jouissant de leur fortune.

C'est sur cette base que j'établis mon calcul. Je divise cette masse de dix millions de contribuables en quatre classes ; chaque classe est divisée en dix sections : d'où il résulte que celui dont la journée est du *minimum* a une action, celui dont elle est du double en a deux, et celui dont elle est du *maximum* en a dix. Le *minimum* et le *maximum* des quatre classes doublent de l'une à l'autre depuis 1 jusqu'à 8. Le *minimum* de la première classe est 1, celui de la seconde classe est 2, celui de la troisième 4, et celui de la quatrième 8, et le *maximum* est 10, 20, 40 et 80. Je comprends dans la première classe le simple journalier qui ne gagne qu'un franc jusqu'à celui qui, par son industrie, ses emplois ou ses revenus, jouit d'une journée de dix francs. Je porte cette classe à cinq millions d'individus, ce qui produit, pour terme moyen de cinq francs, une somme de vingt-cinq millions. La seconde classe, que je porte à deux millions et demi d'individus, dont la journée est de dix à vingt francs, produit trente-sept millions et demi. La troisième classe, d'un million et demi d'individus, dont la journée est de vingt à quarante francs, produit quarante-cinq millions. La quatrième classe, d'un million d'individus, dont la journée est de quarante à quatre-vingt francs, produit soixante millions; ce qui fait, par un tirage, 167,500,000 francs.

Sur cette somme de 167,500,000 francs je prélève cinquante millions pour les lots, dix-sept millions cinq cent mille francs pour les frais, et il reste cent millions de disponibles.

Le nombre d'actions ou de billets serait de cinquante millions; savoir, dans la première classe, vingt-cinq millions; dans la deuxième, douze millions cinq cent mille; dans la troisième, sept millions cinq cent mille; et dans la quatrième cinq millions, qui tous auraient part au tirage de la loterie dans leurs classes respectives.

L'esprit de justice veut qu'on favorise toujours la classe des citoyens la moins fortunée; en conséquence, je divise les cinquante millions pour les lots en quatre parts égales de douze millions et demi : d'où il résulte que les lots de la première classe, dont le produit est de vingt-cinq millions, sont la moitié de la mise; que ceux de la deuxième sont d'environ un tiers ; que ceux de la troisième sont de plus du quart, et que ceux de la quatrième sont de plus d'un cinquième.

Pour procurer un plus grand avantage encore aux classes les plus nombreuses et les moins fortunées, l'on pourrait diviser ainsi les lots : prélever sur la somme de cinquante millions une somme de quinze millions, égale au nombre progressif des mises de chaque classe, diviser la somme restante de trente-cinq millions; ce qui donnerait pour chacune une somme de huit millions sept cent cinquante mille francs; et divisant celle de quinze millions en 1, 2, 4 et 8, ajouter huit à la première, ce qui donnerait 16,750,000 francs; quatre à la deuxième, ce qui donnerait 12,750,000 francs; deux à la troisième, ce qui donnerait 10,750,000 francs; et un à la quatrième, ce qui donnerait 9,750,000 francs. Ce serait plus en rapport avec le nombre des billets distribués dans chaque classe.

Je propose de faire trois tirages de cette loterie; ce qui produirait, pour l'exécution de ce projet dont l'intérêt doit être général, une somme de trois cents millions.

Personne ne serait lésé par cette loterie. L'action la plus forte serait de huit francs, ce qui ferait au *maximum* quatre-vingts francs, et l'on pourrait avoir dix lots. Celui qui serait porté à cette taxe aurait au moins vingt-huit mille livres de revenu; chaque individu prendrait effectivement des billets suivant ce qu'il gagne, ou suivant le revenu dont il jouit; mais la facilité qu'il aurait de pouvoir les vendre avec bénéfice, fait qu'on ne pourrait jamais considérer cette obligation comme un impôt.

L'évaluation faite d'après le tiers d'une population de trente millions d'individus peut être inexacte. La quantité de pauvres peut encore diminuer ce nombre, mais on porterait toujours dans chaque classe le nombre d'actions déterminé. Lorsque les gens inscrits auraient pris leurs billets, on en délivrerait au public, qui, vu le grand avantage de cette loterie, s'empresserait de s'en procurer.

Si cette loterie était divisée en six tirages, les avantages doubleraient; la mise ne serait que de la moitié de la valeur de la journée de travail de chacun, et il y aurait une fois plus de chances à courir. Il résulterait encore l'avantage que le temps des recettes serait plus en proportion avec celui qu'il faudrait employer pour porter ces travaux à leur perfection.

Indication du plan.

A. Place du palais des Tuileries.
B. Monument à ériger à la gloire de l'Empereur.
C. Palais impérial.
D. Palais du Louvre.
E. Galerie du Louvre.
F. Bâtimens à construire.
G. Jardin des Tuileries.
H. Place de la Concorde.
I. Les Champs-Élysées.

1. Fontaines à l'imitation de celles de la place de Saint-Pierre de Rome. — 2. Stylobate formant partie de l'enceinte du cirque, portant des trophées. — 3. Trophées. — 4. Allées. — 5. Grille qui ferme l'entrée du palais. — 6. Colonne triomphale portant des fanaux.

BAUDOUIN, Imprimeur de l'INSTITUT NATIONAL.

Ventose an 13. — (1805.)

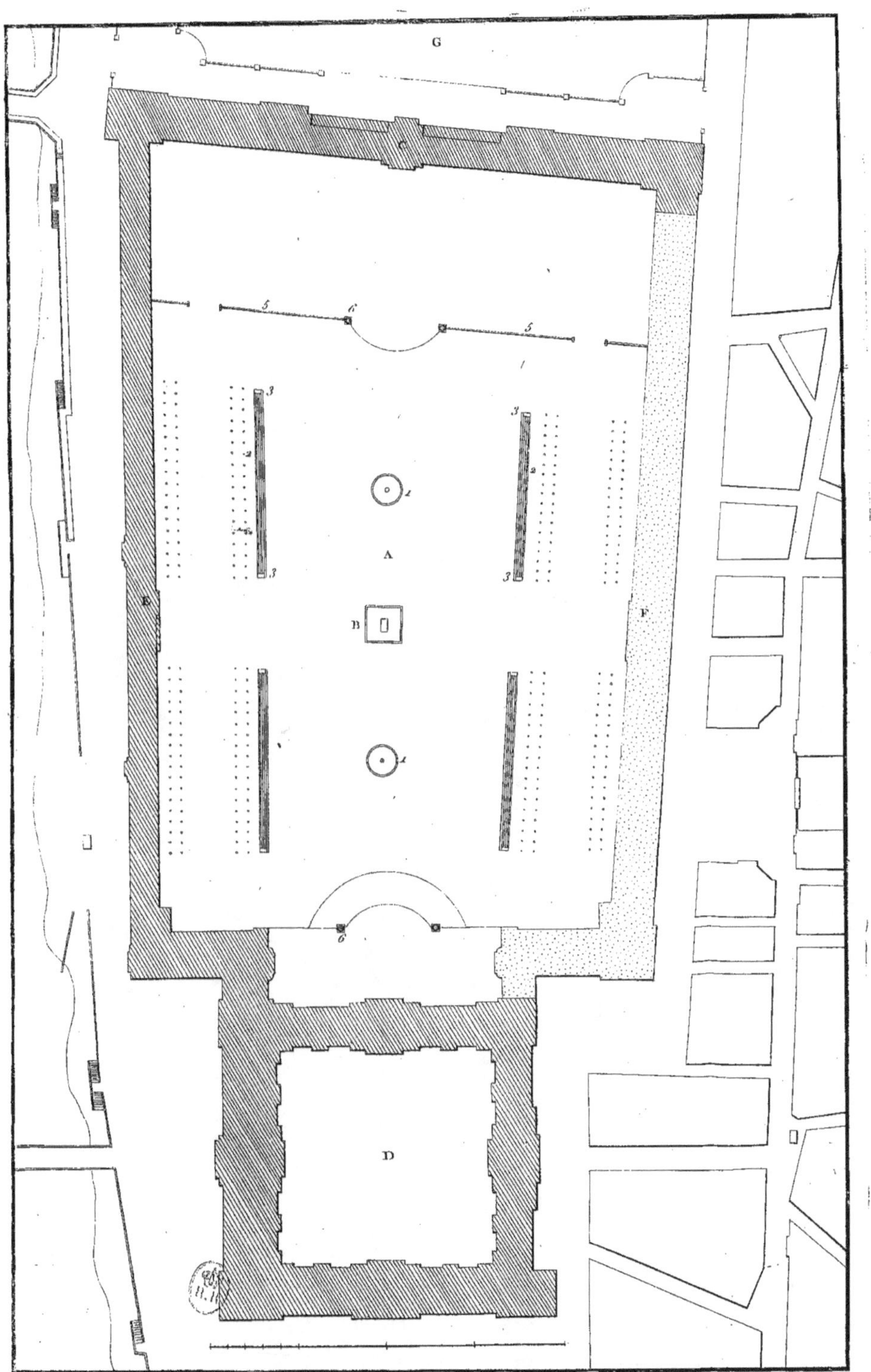

G
C
A
B
D
E
F
1
2
3
5
6

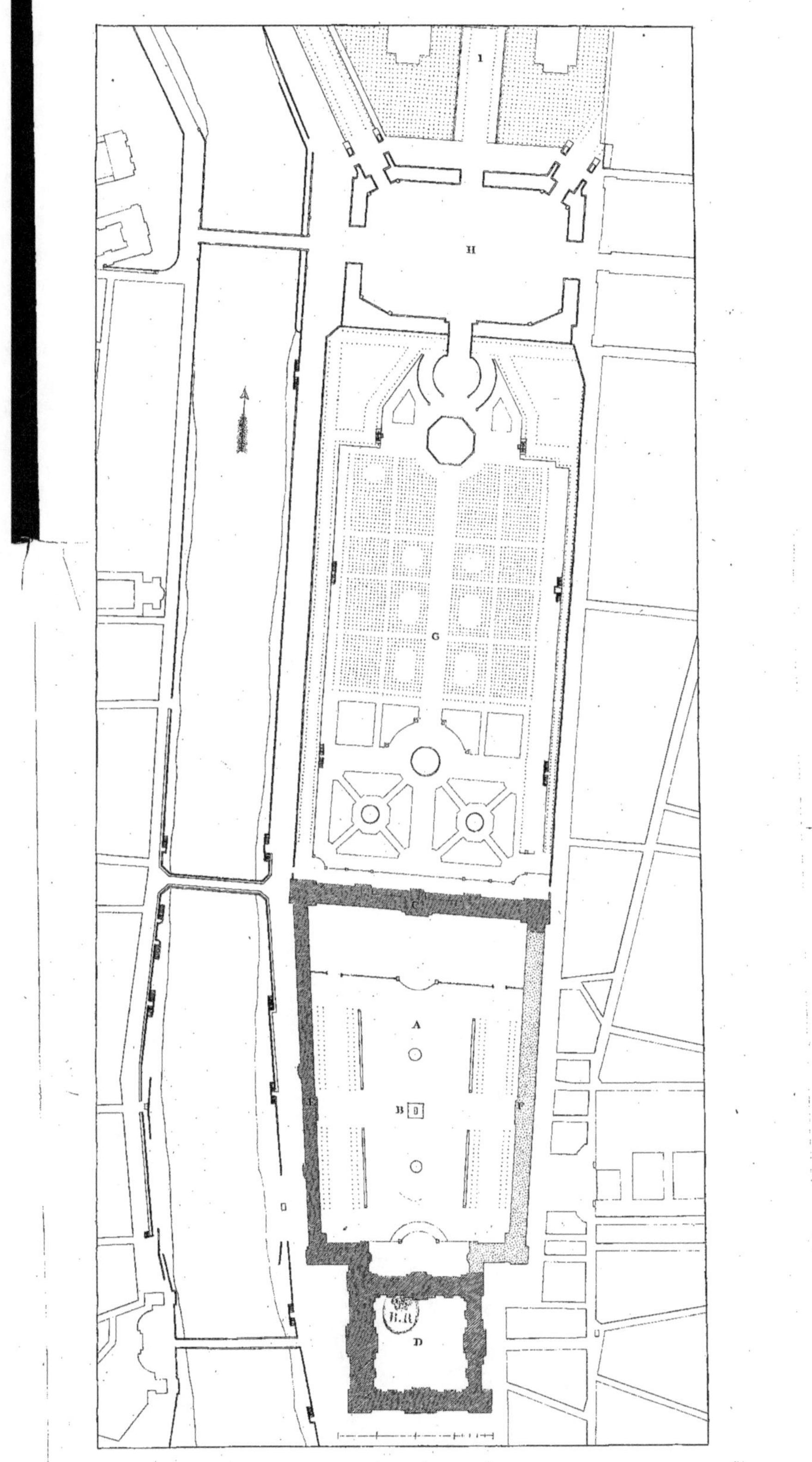

I
H
G
C
A
B
D
D
E
F

COUR D'ASSISES DU HAUT-RHIN.

Présidence de M. le Conseiller **DILLEMANN**.

Audiences des 6 et 7 mai 1864.

PARRICIDE.

TROIS ACCUSÉS.

Joseph Steinkampf, Marie-Anne Steinkampf, sa femme, et Charles Haas.

Des circonstances atténuantes dans leurs rapports avec la peine de mort.

RÉPLIQUE

DE M. LE PROCUREUR GÉNÉRAL DE BIGORIE DE LASCHAMPS.

COLMAR,
IMPRIMERIE DE CH.-M. HOFFMANN, IMPRIMEUR DE LA COUR IMPÉRIALE.
1864.

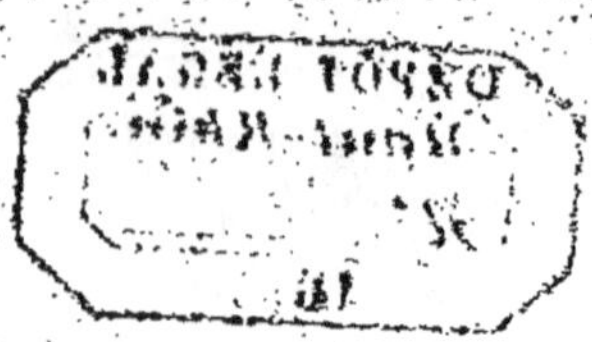